*To my family...for their
constant love and support*

DANNIELLA WESTBROOK

CONTENTS

DANNIELLA WESTBROOK

1
INTRODUCTION

Aggressive behaviour and poor judgement are both classic bipolar traits. When I casually 'sent the boys round' to sort out Kevin in the summer of 2000 I was completely unaware of the disorder, let alone its underlying symptoms.

"Yeah, why not?...do it," I slurred.

Those five innocent words slipped out of the my mouth with ease. I literally thought nothing of it. Even by my standards, giving the nod to rough-up my loyal and faithful fiance was about as low as it gets. My moral compass was always plunging new depths. Earlier that week I also agreed to work in Las Vegas for a friend of a friend who ran an escort agency there.

I'd already told Kevin of my new career path so by that stage I don't think anything would have surprised him. His minders had recently ram-raided their way into our luxury coastal penthouse apartment to collect his belongings. With my knight in shining armour nowhere to be seen and refusing to take my calls, what was the UK's most notorious cocaine addict supposed to do? I was no longer in *EastEnders*...no longer a famous soap star involved in dramatic storylines. This was not scripted. This was the real world and by now my own life story was even more chaotic and unbelievable than half of the residents of Albert Square put together.

Minicab drivers were fuelling my latest stint of psychosis. The poor sods unwittingly delivered half an ounce of coke to me every other day, wrapped in freshly laundered clothes, supposedly collected from my 'ironing lady' in south London. Horrified that my front door had been kicked off its hinges, a glamorous neighbour had dreamt up my new American adventure via a family connection, and was now offering the services of her gangster boyfriend too. And this guy was serious, making most of the so-called hard men I'd hung around with in south London seem like extras from a Danny Dyer film. He didn't drink, he didn't sniff and taking someone out...of the equation...anyone's equation...was all in a day's work to him.

Months later I was famously papped with a huge hole in my nose, an iconic mug shot that will follow me forever. By then Kevin had graciously taken me back. Not before he had received a phone call about what was heading his way, though. Word thankfully reached him via various underworld sources that the heaviest of hard men was en route and common sense somehow prevailed. Thankfully!

I've never spoken about that incident or the Vegas escort agency before, and I'm eternally grateful neither materialised. When I was using cocaine anything was possible. Both those revelations are maybe more shocking than many of the lurid stories in my first book *The Other Side Of Nowhere,* but it's not a competition. Taking cocaine during labour in 1994 and single-handedly destroying my septum are obviously both right up there in terms of humiliation, but until now I've never got to the root of why I continued to take coke for so long...why I was still taking it five years later when I fell pregnant again, and why I tested my relationship with Kevin to the limit on so many occasions.

In July 1999 I had returned to *EastEnders,* for a third spell on the BBC soap that made my name. I was desperately trying to conceal the hole in my nose from the make-up girls, the production staff and the camera crew. I was in no condition to be attempting a comeback on the BBC's flagship TV show so when a fairy Godfather walked into my life I jumped at the chance to leave the soap again. I was sure I could have much more fun on Kevin's arm, taking cocaine and enjoying the influence he had.

Up until now I haven't revealed the sheer depths of my addiction, the paranoid psychosis that has underpinned my life or the harrowing events that meant I could never escape the fall-out of my life with drugs. When writing the last book Kevin's company Premier was a high profile central London dispatch, transport and VIP protection business, turning over £30m a year. That limited what we could and couldn't say about my lifestyle and, as importantly, his...how Kevin became so influential in underworld circles.

Premier's downfall at the height of the credit crunch in 2008 not only helped shaped our future, but also defined our past, bringing us closer than we had ever been before. Then when we found God in LA we were able to put many of our demons to rest. There was, and still is, one massive event that has haunted me since the early '90s, which until now I have never been able to get past, or to deal with properly. It almost certainly prolonged my cocaine addiction for the best part of seven years, and has held me back on every front, especially where Kevin was and is concerned.

My life has been splashed across the tabloid newspapers ever since I can remember. The fact I used cocaine during my entire pregnancy with Kai, and even while I was in labour at the hospital, is well-known. In late 2012 I went on a special edition of The Jeremy Kyle Show and talked candidly about it. These revelations were splashed all over the red-tops again and their associated websites as if they were new exclusives when in reality I had already talked about them.

I'll never be able to shake off the tag of being an irresponsible mother, particularly because of what I put Kai through, but the harsh reality is that I have to deal with those actions and decisions and their consequences from my turbulent life on a daily basis.

There's so much I haven't told about my past, mine and Kevin's lifestyle when we met, and of course everything since the last book concluded almost ten years ago in 2004.

When I finally quit cocaine in Arizona in 2001 I was diagnosed as being on the bipolar spectrum, a disorder which affects your moods, and was known in the past as manic depression. Ecstatic that I had apparently beaten my biggest demon, I dismissed this latest diagnosis out of hand as convenient jargon. However, as I've continued to suffer from the effects of both extreme highs and lows, I came to question this. Just how much of my life with cocaine was self-medication to deal with the 'major life events' that can trigger symptoms of bipolar disorder in the first place?

My first book was offered to me via a literary agent, and I received an advance payment from the publishers in the process. Sure it was good to help people understand about addiction, but it was much more of a business thing, like anything back then. I initiated and funded this autobiography myself. As well as picking up from where we left off in 2004, I needed to delve back into darker periods from the timeline too. In hindsight, if I had realised I would go into as much detail as I have, then I probably wouldn't have done the book at all. When going through this process I've simply had to switch off at times, try and desensitise myself from the content, and that's ironically been my coping mechanism for so long.

We did have interest from publishers along the way, but self-publishing this book ourselves was the only way I thought it would be as transparent as possible.

We all have to move on, and with this new book I hope I can finally do that. As an addict, the battle to stay clean is a constant one and you end up counting the true mates you have left on one hand. Sadly, many bridges are burned along the way. The family members and confidants you both betray and befriend are tested to the limit. Relationships are destroyed. Few survive.

And sometimes that's just the way it goes, because at some point you have to own both your past and your destiny. Some people are prepared to forgive and forget, and understand the way you acted. Others just can't accept the horrible things you said and did. The best way they can deal with things is to bury you firmly in their past, and move on.

Now me, Kevin, and the kids need to move forward in a way we have never been able to do before. I've been nowhere on many occasions. I've come back to *The Other Side Of Nowhere*. Now, we are all hopefully heading somewhere we've never been before....with *Faith, Hope and Clarity*.

2

TWO WORLDS COLLIDE

If I hadn't modelled and acted from a young age and got the part in *EastEnders* when I was 16 I'm sure I would have met a bloke locally, settled down and had a kid. As a child, I appeared in adverts for Asda, Weetabix and Coca Cola and became the face of High Street chain Tammy Girl. I acted in the golden era of BBC kids drama *Grange Hill*, and appeared alongside Freddie Mercury in the video for Queen's Invisible Man when I was 14. It feels like I've been in the spotlight ever since.

From the age of eleven I travelled from my home in Loughton, Essex to Marylebone each day to The Sylvia Young Theatre School. I was used to leaving my comfort zone, and loved commuting in and out of central London. My love of clubbing soon took me further afield, and usually with new friends I had made at Sylvia Young.

Essex has always been known for its nightlife. When I was a kid Tots in Southend and Hollywood in Romford were the big places to go, and I managed to blag my way into both clubs in my mid-teens, years before I was legally allowed. When I was 15 I had progressed to places like The Ritzy in Tottenham and started doing the local circuit with my friends from Woodford and Loughton...Charlie

Chans on a Wednesday, Epping Forest Country Club on Thursday, The Villa (which is now Faces) on Fridays, and maybe a trip up town on a Saturday night to Legends in central London. Then it was always Splash outside by the pool at the 'Country Club' on a Sunday night.

Great times, great parties, but I also wanted to do all the raves too, and was always happy to drive once I'd passed my test. Without the internet, it was a case of getting your pager out, meeting in service station car parks on the M25 and listening to pirate stations like Centreforce to find out where you were heading for the night. Magical times.

My south London friends from stage school were clubbing all over town so I started going out with them more, to the West End to places like The Gas Club or Tommy Mac's Black & White parties where DJs like of Brandon Block were on their way to becoming as famous as footballers or soap stars. I was now the latter, playing Sam Mitchell in *EastEnders*, and with only four TV channels an easily recognisable face on the club scene. We went up to a Boys Own party in Bognor in the early 90s at the height of Sam and Ricky Butcher's relationship. We were staying at Butlins and, coincidently, Mike Reid, who played Ricky's dad Frank, was doing a stand-up show there. I came flying through the campsite on the back of someone's scooter, with an ironing board under my arm...like you do. Mike spotted me and, in that booming cockney voice of his, shouted: "Oi!" as we sped off. It was hilarious.

I even drove us all up to the Hacienda in Manchester once. It's obviously all a bit of a blur, but I look back at these as some of the happiest times of my life, and an era when the drugs I took were still on a recreational basis.

With Kevin being six years older than me, when he started going out in his teens in the south London suburbs in the mid-80s, it was standard to head to the local disco, try to pull a bird and have a fight. You couldn't accept a slow dance at the end of the evening because you might get beaten up, and then you went to the kebab shop to try and have another fight.

By the time the Ministry Of Sound opened in 1993 Kevin had a lot of clubland connections. A doorman that worked there was due to help him collect some 'outstanding debts' after his shift one Sunday morning. Kevin went along to the club to pick up his pal and, while he waited for this guy to clock off, wandered inside the venue. He couldn't believe what he saw, much like anyone who witnessed those sorts of clubs in action for the first time. He was so blown away by it all that he was back there the next week as a punter, and soon taking Ecstasy tablets. Within months he was hooked...taking as many as ten in a single night. But as much fun as he was having, Kevin now looks back and believes that's when his own life imploded.

As well as the Ministry his favourite nights were places like the Drum Club at the Soundshaft behind Heaven in Charing Cross, The Aquarium in Old Street and parties at Bagleys and The Cross in Kings Cross. However, Kevin felt he quickly went from the happy-go-lucky side of clubbing to the dark side of rave, and that was largely because of the people he knew and those he started hanging around with. As well as the celebrities he worked with, through the chauffeur and protection side of his business, there were also celebrated hard men. The more drugs consumed the bigger the comedown. Psychosis, as we both now know it, was everywhere.

Everyone and everything was changing. Lots of people Kevin knew wanted to make money out of clubland, and more and more drugs were taken in the process. While Kevin liked his pills more than his coke, I was obviously totally about cocaine. I don't like the monged, or sedated, feeling pills give you, I much prefer being pranged, or wired. We were chalk and cheese in some respects. Kevin didn't understand why over time I preferred clubs like Browns and I never really got clubs like the Ministry. I mean, drinking out of plastic cups? What's that all about?

Kevin set up his own transport company in the late '80s at the age of 24, above a book shop next to Waterloo Station and built up his business very quickly. As well as transport, cars and couriering, he moved into the world of debt collecting, and came across all sorts of characters along the way. Kevin took on more VIP protection work, ran the doors at a couple of venues in central London, and naturally ended up mixing a lot of business with a lot of pleasure. Kevin met Dave Courtney in the early nineties and a kind of uncle/nephew relationship began.

Dave was surrounded by a lot of colourful characters, and the people Kevin associated with were getting crazier by the minute, the more they immersed themselves in the club business, and the more drugs became involved. But Dave gave Kevin a lot of advice, and they always looked out for each other. Kevin had always been craving a father figure, due to his difficult relationship with his own dad. Kevin believed Dave was the only person who could see through his own fantasy world. The pair of them went to Marbella and Monaco together. They had some wild old times, but Dave also got Kevin to calm things down when it was needed as well.

It was that era in the mid-'90s when the lads mags were massive, and 'celebrity gangsters' even had their own columns. Front magazine did a three-page feature on Kevin at one point. They took him out shooting for the day, and bigged up his apparent gangster lifestyle, which is so ridiculous looking back. But then we both have a diploma in ridiculous.

Kevin had a reputation by then as a 'problem solver' and was very capable of looking after himself. Many associates had access to guns. It's crazy looking back now, but for them at that time it seemed normal. I had seen it all through my extreme drug addiction, and because of the harrowing situations I had found myself in. By the time he met me Kevin had his fingers in all sorts of pies, but had so many people around him that he couldn't get into a fight if he tried. We first got to know each other through my old buddy Michael Greco, who played Beppe di Marco in *EastEnders*. It was at a boxing event at Lancaster Gate Hotel Kevin was co-promoting with Joey Pyle Jnr in November 1999. I knew from the first time he spoke to me and smiled at me that Kevin was the one. He rocked my world immediately and instantly made me feel like I was worth something. When we met that night, Kevin melted my heart. He was cool, calm and handsome, and he had power, all of which was hugely attractive to me.

But Kevin had a softer and caring side too. He offered me immediate emotional support for an impending court case with my ex-husband Ben Morgan, who I famously married weeks after meeting him at a petrol station.

Looking back, Kevin would describe himself then as a "flash fucker" with a lot of money, and loads of hard men working for him. If certain situations needed to be sorted out, then they would be, and I liked that. I needed that. My mum said to me: "What's going on? You're from Loughton and Kevin's from south London. He drives around in a blacked-out Mercedes. Be careful." And it was a bit like Goodfellas. If Kevin had a meeting in the West End, two guys would turn up in a Merc, and take me to him. There was always a car waiting downstairs for me or us. When we arrived at a club, toilets would be emptied for our entourage.

Even Steve McFadden, who plays Phil Mitchell in *EastEnders*, said: "You're not going out with him." As usual, when he gave me some unwanted advice, I replied: "Steve, you do know you're not my real brother, don't you?" Kevin and I clearly weren't the ideal couple or a popular match for a lot of people, but Kevin reckons God smashed our heads together and told us to get on with it, and sort each other out. It soon became clear Kevin would be taking the lead.

Kevin knew I was using coke. I was notorious for it, after all, but then so was he and everyone around him. He just didn't know quite how much I was taking, like so many close to me over the years. By the end of the boxing event Kevin had told me he was going to marry me. This was a man who had just come out of a six year marriage, with a younger daughter of his own, Jordan, pledging to look after me and my boy, and clearly making one hell of a bold statement. From that point on Kevin treated me like a princess, and he adored Kai.

Over the previous month or so I had been hanging around crack houses in Deptford. Now I'd met this guy, who ran the doors at central London venues, and fronted glamorous events. But Kevin wasn't interested in going to clubs that much now. Unlike others around me, he wasn't excited about being papped. He much preferred it if we stayed at home watching movies in bed or went out for lovely meals, and over time that's how our relationship was cemented.

Within a couple of weeks Kai and I had moved into Kevin's penthouse flat in Tower Bridge. I was renting a house in Goffs Oak in Hertfordshire, and still had the lease on it for a couple of months, but I wasn't going to look this gift horse in the mouth. Most appealing was the thought of living with a strong independent businessman who wasn't looking to sponge off me. Compare that to me and Kai living on our own, and there was no contest. There were obviously various other huge perks too. Soon, I was lunching with Kevin most days at Langan's Brasserie, spending the rest of the afternoon at Selfridges on his plastic. With this opulent lifestyle I was in my element, but in no hurry to turn my back on drugs.

Millennium Eve was looming, a momentous occasion, but whether Kevin and I would make it to the year 2000 was debatable. Our high-octane relationship was fragile at best, and there were so many reasons why it shouldn't work. Apart from anything, we never seemed to get any quality time together on our own. With Kevin's apartment perfectly positioned next to Tower Bridge, every Tom, Dick and Harry would visit us on a daily basis.

We were also a prime location for the huge Millennium firework display planned on the Thames. We invited a select few, around 15 friends, to join us for a discreet gathering. Once word got around, however, everyone and their uncle wanted a piece of the action. There must have been around 150 people passing through in the end, enjoying the endless supply of lobster, champagne and cocaine.

Tony Lambrianou came with a few pals. He had been a good friend to Kevin over the years, and had also hosted my 18th birthday with Charlie Kray at The Spencer's Arms in Hornchurch, Essex. Don't ask me how all that came about, because I really can't quite remember. Tony was a larger than life character, and had always looked out for both Kevin and I, so he was very welcome on the night. Other guests included Joey Pyle Snr.

Just like our relationship so far, this New Year's Eve party was bizarre to say the least. Heaving at the seams, I was worried all night that the balcony would collapse, there were so many people trying to get outside to see the fireworks. The party must have shook the whole apartment block. One of our more refined neighbours appeared at the front door, holding a cigarette butt in a pair of tweezers. I'd say that was the least of their worries. Tony - who worked for The Krays, and took a 15 year sentence for his troubles - was a few yards away, and this guy was asking us to quieten things down. It was certainly lively in there, but I spent most of the night crying in the bedroom, which was quite fitting as I'd spent so much of the '90s either locked away in my bedroom or sobbing or both. I'm simply not a fan of big crowds, or socialising with a lot of people all at once.

Kevin's cocaine intake by that stage could hardly be described as recreational, but it was still sociable. My addiction had long been sociable. If we weren't alone together I always threw my toys out of the pram and insisted I wanted to go home to the house I was renting in Goffs Oak. Now I had Kevin, I wanted him all to myself. He was interested in who I was and what made me tick, and I found that amazing...a whole new experience.

However, because this fledging new relationship was being played out while we both depended on drugs - one of us more than the other, of course - there were a lot of grey areas to overcome. As much as Kevin didn't understand me hanging around all the rougher parts of south London, I didn't see him as a gangster, as others did. But like he took me on, I took him on too.

Within days of meeting Kevin I was driving to Tesco in a Porsche Boxster he had given me. I also had round-the-clock protection on tap and full access to a chauffeur, if I needed one, which was most evenings. I know Kevin was desperate to protect me. He says he suddenly had something in his life that he didn't want to lose. Almost instinctively he knew he needed to get out of 'the game' he was in...and reckoned I "turned him soft" overnight. Leaving his lifestyle and those who frequented it would not be easy...or instant either.

While I had been addicted to cocaine for the most of the '90s, for a period Kevin had been caning the pills just as badly. Boozing all day had literally become a way of life for him too. The headquarters of his company Premier were based in Union Street, not far from the South Bank, just down the road from the book shop in Waterloo where his operation had begun. Kevin spent so much time in the Union Jack pub across the road from his offices that he eventually bought it. However, now he says there was someone to come home to.

My coke intake was up to worrying levels, though. It's painful looking back, but I know with Kevin around I abused drugs even more. Cocaine was making me so volatile, something I'm not proud of, and my judgement was all over the place. Kevin even tried to sort out some old debts for me. Boy, how I could have done with him in the past. More than he could ever imagine.

Kevin managed to retrieve my Rolex watch, used to pay off a crack dealer on a local council estate. He bought a female dealer back to the pub once to get to the bottom of another of my dubious transactions. I'd traded in various pieces of jewelry for a load of coke, and when Kevin emptied out her handbag he found my Cartier bangle, some Chanel earrings, a couple of rings and another Rolex. All items I happily handed over to get my fix. Later, on one of our breaks, I swapped the £18,000 Tiffany engagement ring Kevin bought me for an ounce of coke worth barely a tenth of that. That one, he wasn't able to track down.

However. we were a long way from engaged yet, and Kevin still had various engagements of his own to negotiate, plus a few more of mine as well. Drug dealers with whom I had four figure debts suddenly turned their attentions to Kevin, who obviously had much more collateral and clout than me. Many of them had long 'ticked' (or advanced) me the drugs, believing my celebrity meant I could pay up eventually. Now there was finally someone on the scene who, in their eyes, could wipe the slate clean and even get me in credit. Kevin knew a lot of people and could theoretically put dealers I owed money to in touch with other people in the business, as a way of paying off my debts, and that was suggested to him on several occasions. He was far from happy at being asked to be a middle man for my sake, though, and fortunately had enough clout to get things sorted his way.

And it wasn't just Kevin protecting me...everyone associated with him also had my back. Kevin's regular and most trusted minder was his personal bodyguard Luc, who he met in a nightclub in Spain, two months before me. They hit it off instantly, and back in London Luc started driving Kevin around. He soon became my minder too, ferrying me around the West End most days, and quickly dubbed me 'Gucci'. He used to call Kevin

"Gadaffi". Luc was someone both I and Kevin placed our full trust in.

I may have been using a hell of a lot of cocaine still, and that surely clouded any judgement I had left, but I did still have some standards. Playing Russian Roulette was certainly a step too far for even my devil-may-care attitude. I hadn't moved in long at Tower Bridge, and was in the spare room with Kai while about eight or nine of Kevin's associates were bantering in the front room, chopping up lines, drinking and talking about the various scrapes they'd got into recently. Suddenly I heard someone say: "C'mon? Put the gun down, Danni's in the next room with her kid." Petrified, I peaked into the room and this one guy was literally playing Russian Roulette, spinning the barrel on his gun, as he held it to his head...pulling the trigger randomly.

If this nutter was on a death wish, and I appeared to still be on one, then Kevin definitely wasn't anymore. He told everyone they had to go home. All these big lumps suddenly went quiet and, one by one, traipsed out of the flat. They were visibly shocked that the fun and games were over.

So with our new relationship precarious, at best, there were daily dramas and traumas to tackle, as we tried to work out whether this unlikely union would work, who we were and whether we had a future, both individually and together. Kevin was used to my chaos, because up until that point his entire adult life had been filled with his own dramas. I was in all sorts of trouble before we met. Even though Kevin's wealth allowed me to carry on taking drugs initially, him being in my life did at least mean I could look past it, and try to think about building a future...just not yet, unfortunately, without cocaine.

When I was on coke I could be super confident, strutting around the place, and Kevin said he found that attractive at times, but then I would suffer these amazing lows, because I was just too pranged out. I now know it is likely those extreme highs and lows were symptoms of bipolar, but there was little hope of anything like that being diagnosed while I was out of my head all the time. Kevin talks a lot now about psychosis, the effects of drugs and alcohol...whatever it may be that is causing you to act irrationally, or to have lost touch with reality. He reckons his own psychosis had been dominant for eight years, but that it had slowed down since he met me. He had realised he wasn't a gangster and was trying to convince me I wasn't Sam Mitchell.

There is a lot that I haven't told about Kevin's life up until now, but there are also loads of myths about him too...that his fortune was built on drugs and that he had people killed. This is simply not true. Sure, he did a few bad things, and it only takes a few of those for loads of others to be made up. There were tales of him walking into pubs, brandishing shot guns, but that never happened.

At times he wore the 'gangster' badge very well, but not any more. Looking back, Kevin reckons the underworld at that time was, if anything, fairly harmonious. He is quick to remind anyone getting too carried away to consider how much money was being made in those days. The rave and club scene was good to a lot of people in London at that time, so if it wasn't broken, there was no need to fix anything. In reality, in Kevin's world, reputation counted for so much, and more often than not a problem was solved with a phone call. The right words or an apology could sort out most issues.

DANNIELLA WESTBROOK

3
A POTENT MIX

Kevin and I getting together was clearly a potent mix - a coked-up washed-up celebrity meeting a pilled-up, hyped-up businessman. Throw in some of south London's most influential people and leave to simmer.....then explode!

So many people were taking cocaine at that time, especially anyone connected to certain circles. I was able to hide my extreme addiction fairly easily. Those you're with think you're only doing gear with them, not with everybody you meet, 24-7, each and every day. Like most, Kevin didn't know just how big a cokehead I was. When we lived down on the coast, he hadn't a clue taxi drivers were collecting half ounces of coke from my so-called ironing lady in London...delivering it straight to my front door 100 miles away. I was relentless. When Kevin did go to sleep, I'd simply creep back out of bed and carry on sniffing.

Somehow, after years of cocaine abuse, I was still able to consume amazing volumes of the drug, and function the next day. Now with Kevin on my arm, telling me he'd always be there for me, I felt invincible. Maybe my new-found sense of security helped carried me further along the path to ultimate destruction.

I loved the power that came with Kevin. I could be as flash as I wanted. If we were in clubs where his security worked I could cause trouble and start fights. I could always get into most clubs easily anyway...now I could get people thrown out of them on a whim too. If someone was sitting in the VIP room where I wanted to be, I'd make sure they were turfed back out into the main club. It was horrible, but I was horrible. There were always fireworks when I was with Kevin and I loved it.

To some extent when he met me, Kevin had been there and done it all before me, so he didn't try and put me down for what I was doing, the drugs I was taking. He simply tried to take me through it, in a way tried to get it out of my system. He understood why I did certain things, and to understand a crazy person, you've got to be a bit crazy yourself, I guess. Kevin believed that if he wasn't there for me, in whatever condition I was in or whatever limits I was pushing my body and life to, that I may not make it. He loved me, and simply found it hard to walk away. We have split up temporarily on many occasions. Thank God we always got and do get back together.

Kevin says he fell in love with me instantly too but his therapist was always asking him: "Are you her lover or her father?" In a very short space of time he did become Kai's dad, though. There was no question about that. It was a huge responsibility, but he embraced it. He had his own daughter a couple of years older than Kai and whatever was going on his personal or private life we always put them first, or at least we thought we did. Increasingly, Kevin was putting all of us first.

The one thing Kevin and I did have in common was that we were aggravation junkies. It seemed, for me, the more chaos I could cause, the better. When we first met, if someone was on their way to confront Kevin, he was like "yeah, bring it on". It was like the guy had no fear, and that was massively attractive too.

Kevin reckons I was first person in his life to upstage him. I was cheeky, outrageous and, for him, fun. Kevin says that when he met me, I supersized him in the drama stakes. Not many people could handle me, but Kevin could, and he got off on that. I was up to no good, a known drug-addict off the telly. He had just left his wife of six years and it seemed for a while that the bigger the drama the bigger the buzz we both got. And there was plenty of drama.

We became a tight unit overnight. Kevin is a man of his word...old school...and he looked after me from day one. I felt so lucky. If we were in a room full of people, or in a bar or a club, we would spend the entire night together. It felt like we were the only people there.

Three weeks after our chance meeting at the boxing event, Kevin whisked me off to Orlando. It was all expenses, VIP treatment, the lot, and he promptly got down on one knee in the first class cabin and proposed. It was an emphatic 'yes' from me, but then I do have a history of compulsive marriages. When we arrived in Florida it was perfect, everything laid-on, six-star luxury all the way. Interestingly, I never used coke when I went abroad. It was as if I left that part of me back in London, and was able to get off on the buzz of being in another country. Maybe, subconsciously all my issues remained at home. Sure, it obviously wasn't as easy to get hold of any gear outside of London and the UK, but not impossible. I don't know why, but I've never been on a girls holiday to Majorca or been to Ibiza to party with friends, so the thought of taking drugs abroad really is alien to me.

When I was away, the fact that I could drop coke just like that, for a few days or a week...sometimes a fortnight...did give me hope that one day I could knock it on the head completely. That's not to say that I wasn't gagging for a line by the time I got home. I could usually be found towards the end of any trip plotting how I was going to get some as soon as we landed.

In Orlando, with my new man, I was like a pig in muck - shopping to my heart's content at designer stores in The Florida Mall. I thought I had died and gone to heaven, when in reality my drug addiction should have already killed me.

A couple of days into the trip, as was usual during the early days of our relationship, something was up. Kevin was pacing up and down in our hotel suite as he spoke to someone from London on the phone. There had been a problem with a doormen who worked for the security company Kevin owned, and it needed immediate attention. We were on the next plane home. Kevin asked me if I minded, and I said as long as I can have one more afternoon at The Florida Mall, it was all good with me. In any case, I had to get back to film what would be my latest round of final scenes at *EastEnders*, and would never shun any chance to reacquaint myself with my favourite white powder.

It's a pity I couldn't let go of cocaine at this point, that I couldn't see the potential of a wonderful relationship with Kevin. We were each single parents, both divorced...on paper a perfect match. Kevin was slowly coming around to a cleaner and less salubrious lifestyle, but he was five years older than me and, he would argue, a lot wiser too! On the other hand, I was still way out there, seemingly keen to live up to my hell-raising reputation at the flick of a switch. As much as anything, I had developed a worrying addiction to drama. The actress in me was never far away, always intent on auditioning for the lead role on a daily and weekly basis.

Back in London I was at my drama queen best while Kevin was in hospital having a hiatus hernia operation. It was last thing he needed, given everything going on around him, but he was booked in for the op and Luc was under strict instructions to guard him at his bedside, particularly as I was roaming around town clubbing...as usual, off my head.

Kevin had just come out of four and a half hours of surgery at the Princess Grace Hospital in the West End, and desperately needed to recuperate. He had given a friend the unenviable task of following me around the West End. If I could be contained in town, and preferably kept away from the safe confines of his private room at the hospital, then all well and good. The hospital staff had set up a bed for Luc next to Kevin, as regular reports of my movements filtered back to him. Flitting from place to place, I was on my usual circuit - Titanic, Ten Rooms and the Atlantic Bar - and I certainly kept Kevin's mate on his toes. I always had a chauffeur driven Mercedes S-Class waiting outside, so it was easy for me to get about.

The feedback that night was positive. Everything seemed relatively calm...for me...so encouraged by those updates Kevin dropped off to sleep. When he woke several hours later, at around 3.30am, Luc had nodded off too and I was stood at the end of his bed, feeling wide-eyed and bushy-tailed. Kevin, on the other hand, says I looked vacant, dead to the world and crazed, all at the same time. He was horrified and said I reminded him of another famous addict, Ginger, the character Sharon Stone played in the Martin Scorsese film, *Casino*. His first thought, as I stared at him manically, saying nothing, was "I'm fucked!" He said there was an eerie silence, and it was as if time stood still as my eyes fixed on him. I think he was literally pinching himself to see if this was all some kind of bad dream. Fortunately, for him, the nightmare was over as quickly as it started. I dropped a letter I'd written on his chest, and walked out. The note explained that I thought the world of him, and apologised for not visiting him as much as I should have, that I desperately wanted to kick drugs, and make a go of our relationship, adding that I should have been there for him more.

Kevin woke Luc and explained what had just happened. Luc was having none of it and said: "Gucci hasn't been here mate. You're on morphine. You're hallucinating." When Kevin showed Luc the note I'd left he looked mortified and rushed down to reception to ask how the hell I'd managed to get in. The answer was that I walked in through the front door, past the nurses on reception and straight to Kevin's bedside. I knew where he was. I had visited a few times before, just hadn't popped in at that time on a Sunday morning before, dressed-up to the nines, totally worse for wear.

More worrying for Kevin, was what I was up to now, and he was right to be worried. Back at the apartment, I decided to grace the balcony with an impromptu show...seven floors up! One minute I was sitting there happily snorting more coke, the next I had ripped off my dress and, wearing just a thong and swigging from a bottle of Dom Perignon, was teetering on the edge of the balcony rail, as various people returned home from their night out. I was screaming like a banshee. Fortunately Kevin's pal, who had caught up with me again by now, was able to drag me down and back inside to safety.

As usual, I rarely helped myself in the drama stakes. I was a well-known junkie, but sometimes the stick I got was relentless. Iain Lee, the presenter of *The 11 O'Clock Show* on Channel 4, loved poking fun at me. The popular satirical programme, which launched the likes of Ali G and Ricky Gervais, joked each night about various topical issues and celebrities currently in the public eye. However, one night it went too far. They flashed up a picture of Kai, aged 3, riding his BMX, and referred to him as: "London's youngest drug dealer." Lee also called me a "coked-up slut". I've got no complaints about "coked-up" - clearly - but the term 'slut' is way out of line. Lee later confirmed in a newspaper article that he called me a "slut", adding: *"Yes, it was pretty harsh, I suppose, but that was kind of the point of the show. I then started getting threats from somebody connected to her, I think."*

Kevin took as much of this chaos and high-profile criticism in his stride as he could, his own dramas never too far away, but the strain was starting to tell. As the intensity of both Kevin's lifestyle and our hi-octane relationship heightened, my behaviour became more and more erratic. Maybe this whirlwind romance had simply happened too quick? Maybe we weren't meant to be together after all? It was as if we had both quickly got over each other...me the dark side of Kevin's business, and he the even edgier side of me. Kevin decided we should move to the south coast. Suddenly, running around town with me wasn't so appealing and, in fact, becoming more detrimental to his business and professional life by the day.

We just didn't seem to have any time on our own in town. Luc was now living in Kevin's apartment too, and we just didn't have the space we needed, the quiet nights to sit and watch a DVD together, like most couples would. People Kevin worked with would turn up at all times of the night, supposedly to discuss business, but usually to see if Kevin wanted to pop out for a drink. The office being so close, as well as so many of the skeletons from my past, also meant escaping to the coast seemed an ideal opportunity. A great idea if we had both stopped using, but not when we were still acting like lunatics.

Moving meant we were only running away from ourselves, as I had done on so many occasions before. Kevin calls these moves a 'geographical'...supposedly moving away at the right time for the right reasons. He may have thought he wanted to get away from London, but being so far away from my regular dealers wasn't at all ideal for me. It did make sense to move away from town, to step aside from it all, and try and carve out a new life somewhere else, where our relationship could be nurtured, not nullified. However, neither of us really wanted to be down on the coast. Kevin because of his business and me because of my addiction and the hustle and bustle of the central London club life and designer boutiques I thrived on.

Kevin was doing loads of coke still, but mainly at the weekends, and the odd week day. Meanwhile, I was at it non-stop, and always started each day with a line. The whole thing was self-perpetuating. Kevin stayed in town more, because of work, and because he didn't want to come home on a Monday, Tuesday or Wednesday night and watch me getting smashed. The more I moaned at him being in town, the more he stayed away and the more coke I did on my own. That's when I started having cocaine seizures. They're like epileptic fits, and leave you shaking on the floor. Poor Kai was still only a toddler, and would feed me Mars Bars as I lay there, to try and revive me. I still can't believe I put myself or my young son in that position. Over the years I have had to take responsibility for a whole host of harrowing moments in my life. Some are easier to own than others.

4

DIVA LAS VEGAS

I had now left Albert Square for the third time. Michael Greco and other co-stars tried in vain to talk me out of leaving, insisting I'd regret it, and that I may never be able to come back again, but I felt no remorse or shame. Unbeknown to almost everyone, I had a huge hole in my nose, and I'd simply grown tired of trying to hide it. In my mind, just leaving *EastEnders* made my life a million times easier.

To try and make a real go of this relatively new relationship, as an engaged couple engaged in all the wrong activities, we moved to a penthouse apartment on the south coast. The move placed an immediate strain on the relationship, because the further Kevin was away from central London the less he was around. My cocaine usage was at a harrowing level, and if Kevin wasn't at home I was free to take as much as I wanted. When he did return we argued loads. Kevin decided to book a suite at his favourite hotel at County Hall on the Thames, nearby to Premier. He was still taking a lot of Ecstasy and using his own fair share of coke...generally working hard and playing harder back in town.

I had come to the attention of a glamorous neighbour, who lived in the same apartment block as us.

She was all fake boobs and tan, very glam and drove a Jaguar XIR. Forever talking about her relatives in Vegas, I don't know what she personally did for a living, and I never asked. I'd not long had more surgery to take my own boobs up to a 34D, and when I wasn't indoors, sniffing coke like it was going out of fashion, or waiting for deliveries from unsuspecting cabbies, I was tearing around in my silver Boxster. I guess we just clicked on a extreme material level, and as she got to know me better, over lunch and shopping trips into town, she heard all about my trials and tribulations and rows with Kevin. But she did only see and hear one side of it all. She would see me upset loads, and then when Kevin decided to stay away for a longer period of time than usual, she casually suggested I get a visa sorted out for the States, and come out with her to Vegas to help her family member run an escort agency there. She was forever showering me with compliments and said I could make a lot of money working as an escort myself.

My situation with Kevin was worsening by the day, with little or no contact. I was a mess and out of control. I would bombard him with phone calls, and the more I called the more he refused to pick up. My record is more than 70 calls in one day, all with their own charming message. By mid-afternoon his answerphone was full, and nobody else could leave a message, which hardly strengthened my case. It's crazy looking back that I acted so manically. Increasingly isolated, I felt out on a limb down on the coast and resented being away from central

London. Kevin didn't look like he was coming round any time soon, and hadn't picked up one of my calls in days.

I was taking coke all night, through the night, every night. The more I did, the more my paranoia intensified. I wasn't sure how long this opulent lifestyle would continue. I'd burned all my bridges at *EastEnders*, so in the depths of my psychosis I began to seriously consider new 'prospects', apparently being handed to me on a plate.

No disrespect to escorts the world over, but these were clearly not the thoughts of a sane and stable person, whether from a moral standpoint, or considering my status. Sure, I wasn't well known in America, but how long could I get away with that, without someone in the UK, and most probably a tabloid newspaper, finding out? Coked up and pranged out, the idea certainly didn't phase me, though. My frequent feelings of worthlessness were constantly clouding my decisions. I'd hung around enough crack dens by then and found myself in enough compromising positions not to be daunted in the slightest at something so seedy.

During one call that Kevin did finally take I excitedly told him about my new vocation, as I hoovered up another large line of gear. I'm sure he didn't believe a word of it, or think that I would go through with it. But I was sure I could do it. I was haggard, but I was still young and I could still scrub up. My friend told me that it was more like being an escort than a prostitute, going out with people for dinner, but, let's face it, there was going to be far more than a slap-up meal involved.

I told Kevin that I was deadly serious, that I wasn't playing him. That was the final straw. He told me he was coming back to collect his Bang & Olufsen stereo and his clothes, and he was officially moving out. So it must have been serious...I mean, collecting his precious state-of-the-art Bang & Olufsen stereo? This guy WAS serious...but then his girlfriend had just told him she was heading to Vegas to become an escort!

However, this was clearly no laughing matter. I then got a message that someone was heading down to the apartment to collect Kevin's stuff. I had obviously hoped Kevin would come himself, and that I could talk him round. I thought we could try and patch things up, but when I found out he wasn't coming I decided it would be hilarious if I was nowhere to be seen, and so called his bluff and headed into London for some retail therapy.

When I returned later that night, I was greeted by my neighbour, flabbergasted that my front door was in tatters, just yards from her own apartment. Let's just say the guy Kevin sent had made his own way into the flat. My friend's boyfriend was less than impressed too. This guy was seriously heavy, probably the heaviest I'd ever come across. I was promptly sat down by the pair of them and asked if I wanted to, as they put it, "call it on".

I was desperate and distraught, believing I was either heading to Vegas to turn tricks or back to Bermondsey

to burn out. I obviously thought I was Dolly Rawlins from the classic ITV drama Widows or something, because I did exactly that. I called it on. What the hell was I thinking? Probably, something along the lines of: "If I can't have Kevin, then nobody can." After years of torment, Kevin was the one person who I thought would look after me, and now he'd had enough too. Sure, I had driven him away, like everybody who'd had enough of me, but more than anything I was still running away from the horrors of my past. I was more like Sam Mitchell than you could imagine. Like she had left Albert Square to become a lap-dancer in Spain, I was heading to the States to join the oldest profession in the world.

This was clearly the work of extreme cocaine psychosis. Every other day I was suffering seizures, convulsions that would leave me laid out on the floor. When I gave the order I didn't think about it again. I was probably more worried about my next hit. I was clearly well out of my league. I'd heard people 'call it on' before in south London, but never saw the results. Fortunately for everyone's sake there was no 'result' on this occasion. On the way down to London this guy and his cohort phoned a few connected people, and eventually got through to a middleman who quickly intervened. Word got through to Kevin, who effectively had to un-send those boys round. Poor sod. I should have been ashamed of myself. It seems incomprehensible now that I could do such a thing, that I stooped so low, but I was so detached from reality, literally anything was possible.

Enough was enough for Kevin, and that I assumed was the end of that. Dropping the Vegas option as quickly as I had disastrously picked it up, I headed to Deptford where a friend had a spare room above a social club. I was still getting all my coke from someone nearby, so it made perfect sense to me...just like the escorting had the week before. Bar the Porsche Boxster, I'd lost virtually everything by now - my loving fiance, my career, and roughly a million pounds, including all the profit from the the sale of my Buckhurst Hill flat. The five star lifestyle Kevin had lavished on me since we'd met had gone, and the middle of my nose had disappeared. I thought "fuck it...I might as well live as near to my dealer as possible."

Bt that stage I really didn't give a shit. I remember waking up one day during this period and seeing Paula Yates had overdosed and died. For a moment I wished it was me. This contrasted massively to my unwavering love for Kai, and, thankfully, it was the thought of leaving him behind that always made me shake myself out of any suicidal thoughts.

Moving in above the social club was yet another demoralising climbdown for me. However, when the chips were down, when I did come crashing back to earth again, as long as Kai was by my side - fed and clothed - and I was as near to cocaine as possible...well, that was genuinely about as much as I thought I could hope for. The feelings that I deserved everything that came my way were so overpowering, that whenever I did end up on my arse again my default setting was to bed down, and take as much coke as I could.

Anxious not to lose any more face with my 'associates' down there, I wanted to get away from the coast as much as Kevin did. I was desperate to try and forget all about that little episode of my life, as I had tried to do on so many occasions before. And so started a familiar pattern, as I tried to woo Kevin back while ensuring my huge coke habit was maintained, now largely without a generous allowance from him. I still had my sports car, my mobile phone and Kevin would send me some money to ensure Kai was looked after, but I would need to get as much gear as possible on tick and hope I was back with Kevin again by the time anyone started to call those debts in.

The squalor in which Kai and I lived in that one room, and the tortured condition my addiction had become was so hard to take. Kevin was always in contact, picking up Kai with Jordan when he could, and I certainly kept in touch...hounding him up to 30 times a day on the phone to take me back...wearing the sexiest outfit I could muster up when he did visit. If anything, trying to impress Kevin enough to be forgiven did mean I had to be on my A-game, and that I had to ease up on my coke intake in the run up to the times he did come and visit, if only momentarily, and maybe that did help keep me slightly in check at times.

Eventually Kevin cracked, and I was on the move again - this time with him, as we headed to a five-bed Georgian house in Datchet, near Windsor. Another 'geographical', if ever there was one. Not south or east. Very much west and outside of central London too. For me it was a case of 'from the sublime to the ridiculous' as I swapped the cramped, dank room above the social club with another taste of Kevin's luxury lifestyle. You literally couldn't make it up.

And I didn't even have to get my hands dirty. With any move like this, Kevin would leave it all to Luc. He found us the place down on the coast, and he found us the house in Datchet. Typically, Luc would come up with three options...just like the TV show *Location Location Location*. He would have 'moved us' out of the penthouse and also 'moved us' into the house in Windsor. I was lucky I was moving anywhere, and that Kevin had decided to forgive me once more.

However, I was up to my old tricks within days of the move to Datchet, attempting to throw myself down the gallery staircase at the house. I was battered on coke again, and arguing with Kevin. He needed to go back to the hospital to have a minor complication with his hernia checked out. I'd been up all night, and wanted to drive him to the hospital. He was rightly having none of it, so as he and Luc walked out of the house, I stumbled down two thirds of the stairs, and then threw myself down all six of the remaining steps. Like the coward I was, I just didn't have the full 'Dynasty' flight in me. It was pathetic, and Kevin and Luc just looked at me in despair, as I lay there on the floor in a heap. Kevin chuckled as he picked me up, and carried me into the front room, put me on the sofa and tucked me up in a quilt, before leaving for the hospital.

I wasn't able to get too comfy in Windsor, though. Clearly perturbed about my mental state, Kevin suggested I check in to The Priory Hospital in Roehampton, south west London, and offered to pay for a 28-day course of treatment for me. By offering to fund my treatment, Kevin had again seen something in me worth saving. God only knows how! This hospital has famously treated a whole host of celebrities for various addictions, bouts of depression and psychotic illnesses.

I still had absolutely no intention of giving up cocaine, but The Priory was as good a place for me as anywhere right now, and again a million miles away from my old digs in the depths of Deptford. In fact, for the most part, the stay there was great for me, and the perfect chance for me to recharge my batteries after an eventful seven or eight months since I had met Kevin. Not many men have to put their new girlfriend into rehab, but not only was Kevin insisting I went, he was happy to pick up the bill too. Shame I could never truly appreciate how lucky I was. The urge to take cocaine again was just always stronger than any objectivity.

I had been papped at the Soap Awards earlier that month in July of 2000, and someone had finally spotted something was missing. In The Priory I couldn't and didn't use cocaine, but one morning I was about to get one hell of a shock when I tuned into the *The Big Breakfast* on Channel 4. There was presenter Johnny Vaughan holding up the front page of *The Sun*, which had my face, minus my septum, plastered all over it. The picture I had dreaded for so long - showing a gaping hole where the tissue and cartilage separating my nostrils should be - had found its way, slap bang on the front of the biggest-selling newspaper in the country, in those days, at the height of its powers with a daily readership of more than ten million.

Johnny was adding to my pain, excitedly showing the paper to millions of *Big Breakfast* viewers, and generally poking fun at me, as was, I'm sure, anyone who saw it. At least the show's co-presenter, my old Sylvia Young pal Denise Van Outen, was trying to stand up for me. Bless her. A couple of years ago I bumped into Vaughan at a function, and ten years or so clean he was visibly shocked at my appearance. I'm not sure if he remembered chuckling to the nation about my plight, but he exclaimed: "Wow, you look different." I mumbled: "Yeah, and you're bald...and there's not a lot you can do about that."

The article in *The Sun* included quotes from the likes of Elton John suggesting therapist to the stars, Beechy

Colclough, could help me, and Kevin thought seriously about contacting him. However, I was making good progress at The Priory, and there was a sense of relief that the secret about the hole in my nose was now out. I felt optimistic about the future and, with Kevin waiting loyally in the wings, the most positive I ever had about our relationship.

DANNIELLA WESTBROOK

5
BACK TO REALITY

When my time was up at the The Priory, encouraged by my successful stint there, Kevin whisked me off to Palm Island in Barbados for a holiday, and I was clean the whole time there. I really was a lucky girl...to be alive and being treated so well by Kevin once again.

Tabloid photographer, Jason Fraser - one of the paps who followed us out to the Caribbean to see if I was clean - was impressed at how well I had behaved and how tight we appeared as a couple. He approached us to do an exclusive shoot, which he could distribute to a whole host of publications and duly put all the rumours of continued turmoil behind us. Jason was a well-known and shrewd pap, who had made his name taking pictures of Princess Diana and Dodi Fayed in the south of France shortly before they both died. We agreed to work with him, and he was right, it did take the heat off us. Upon publication, the rest of the paps left us alone to enjoy our holiday.

However, this was yet another false alarm. My relationship with cocaine was far from over, and on the plane home from Barbados I feigned a toothache so I would need to rush to the dentist as soon as we landed.

I've previously said that Kevin needed to head straight to the Premier offices for a meeting, and that alone I panicked and called a friend who could get me cocaine. The fact was I had an urgent business meeting of my own...a meeting with whichever one of my dealers I could get hold of first. I was desperate for cocaine - clucking, as they say in the trade - and when those feelings engulfed me I went to extraordinary lengths to get it.

When I finally hooked up with Kevin in the early hours, and he saw what state I was in, he wanted nothing to do with me. He was adamant this was finally it, but he didn't want me going back above the social club, he could thankfully see no sense in that, so generously and gallantly put me and Kai up in a town house he was renting in Orpington in Kent.

Kevin had no intention of seeking rehab himself, but his own psychosis was terrible. He was paranoid certain 'businessmen' were trying to use his legitimate company to wash their dirty money. My nose, or lack of it, was all over the papers and the TV, and the longer I stayed pranged out on coke, the straighter Kevin felt he had to become. His own cocaine intake had got so bad that he had developed a worrying problem of his own. Not surprising, I guess, hanging around me so much.

We were on our break, and Kevin had checked into a hotel near to the Union Jack pub, which Luc was now living above. Kevin was in such a bad way that he would often wake up laying at the end of Luc's bed, and not know how he'd got there. He clearly wasn't functioning well at all, and I'm sure my own psychosis wasn't helping. He had always been in to his Ecstasy tablets, but more and more Kevin was banging away at the coke too, probably, if anything, to try and deal with how much I was taking. It was all a million miles away from his formative years and nothing either of us have talked about publicly before.

A lunch meeting at Langan's was the tipping point for him. His mum was dying of cancer and he had an overwhelming sense of doom hanging over him. If he didn't take drastic action, Kevin feared for both of us. Determined to quit his own drug habit, he told anyone close to him not to offer or get coke for him, even if he begged them, and you clearly have a problem if you feel the need to come out with something like that. However, at Langan's that afternoon, while meeting an old colleague, Kevin started on his favourite white wine, Chablis, and then rushed out to the car where he asked an associate to get him some gear. When that person protested Kevin told him to get it or he'd be sacked. When the coke did arrive Kevin rushed downstairs to the toilets, and didn't even make it to a cubicle. He just stood there in the foyer area and sniffed up as much as he could from the wrap in front of him. He looked at himself in the mirror with white powder all over his face and realised, for him, the game was up. He went back upstairs, ordered a bottle of vodka, finished the rest of the gram, then made a call and booked himself into The Priory.

Kevin had the foresight to realise the potential of his problem, something I had never been able to do. He spent 28 days in The Priory, and it gave him time away from everything, including me. It meant he could figure out who he was, not what he had become. For a whole month, he didn't have to play gangsters or be a troubleshooter...nor try and be my dad. Instead, he could take a step back from everything. I, for one, know this can work if you genuinely want to give up whatever vices have put you into rehab in the first place, just like I know rehab is pointless if you're doing it for the wrong reasons. Fortunately, Kevin did want to stop, and deep down I knew one of us had to. When he came out, while he may have pushed the old Kevin to the curb, it didn't mean that everybody had forgotten that version of him overnight. Most people were like "where's Kev, where's the crazy man?"

Kevin was properly on the straight and narrow now, and I envied him for how calculating he was able to be. He knocked the coke, pills and booze on the head just like that, all in one go, and told everyone that he was a born-again Christian, and had found God...long before he actually was and did. But it worked, because everyone backed off him. None of his old cohorts wanted to be around a teetotal and clean bible-bashing convert. Kevin fortunately realised that one of us needed to slow down if we were both to ever have some kind of normality in our life. There were two young kids involved and someone had to get a handle on it all, to try and take control. I wasn't ready for that, but thankfully Kevin was. It would be a rocky ride yet, but at least one of us was on the right track.

When he came out of The Priory in September 2000, Kevin went to stay with his mum, and was at least able to have some quality time with her in those last few months. Not that I cared much. I was being a right old cow, showing little sympathy, and using up to ten grams a day. All this despite the obvious immense shame and huge embarrassment I should have been feeling over the now well-documented gaping hole in my nose. I hadn't learned any lessons, and none from my fiance, who was diligently attending Alcoholic Anonymous meetings, and generally staying sober and clean.

When Kevin was late for an arranged visit to the house in Orpington, because his AA meeting had overrun, I took a handful of painkillers in a desperate cry for attention. When Kevin did arrive at the house I had passed out and there was no answer. He managed to force his way in, and found me spread out on my bed. When he questioned how serious I was I grabbed another handful of pills and swallowed them too. That little trick saw me thrown into the shower by Kevin and then admitted to hospital to get my stomach pumped. Kevin and my family agreed that I would go and stay at my dad's, and by the time I had fully recuperated, the lease in Orpington had run out. I had nearly reached rock bottom.

My father adored Kevin and desperately wanted me to settle down with him, and was doing all he could to help the relationship, but now had a new partner himself, and they had a young daughter together. I couldn't stay with my mother. She had been taught through a recent course of therapy aimed at helping her deal with me, that tough love was the way forward. As much as it pained everyone, I was now staring at another stint back at the social club. I'd done it before, so this time dumbing down like that was a hell of a lot of easier...albeit, equally heartbreaking.

Kevin, meanwhile, was rebuilding his own life, while he nursed his mum in the last few weeks of hers'. And still he considered taking me back...eventually. We started to see each other again, on and off, probably because I had hounded Kevin for weeks and because he wanted to keep an eye on me, or to make sure Kai was OK, more than anything. Somehow that man still saw something worth saving. He would talk to me on the phone for hours, in between my frequent trips in the Boxster to pick up more coke. I'll never understand why he persevered with me.

By now Cheryl Barrymore, then wife of well-known TV presenter Michael, had become my agent...the latest in a long line of people who thought they could save me.

Kai and I spent loads of time at Cheryl's flat, a welcome distraction from the social club, and she more than anyone, encouraged me to try and make my peace with Kevin, insisting it would give Kai the best chance possible of a stable future. I had hidden my cocaine addiction from Cheryl fairly effectively, and on the surface was making progress again. It must have looked like I was doing something right because Kevin even invited me and Kai to live with him again, back at the house in Windsor.

Delighted at the reprieve Kevin had given me, I was determined to clean up my act and make a go of the latest chance he had given me. There was an air of optimism, and for the first time I could remember in years, but it was still massively a case of papering over the cracks. However, the relationship had clearly improved considerably because, a couple of months later in January 2001, I discovered I was pregnant. And although I started this pregnancy still using cocaine all concerned were praying I wouldn't end this one still sniffing away right up to, and during, giving birth.

The truth is that I was still in such a mess, and still craving cocaine. Time and time again in my life, just when I have managed to claw myself back into a winning position, I hit the self-destruct button. On paper, it's incomprehensible why I have self-imploded so many times. If it's not the drugs playing havoc with my decision making, maybe classic bipolar symptoms like poor judgement and feelings of hopelessness combine with catastrophic consequences.

So here we were again. Pregnant and indignant, I started using heavily again, and imploded spectacularly. Kevin was furious, and this time I feared we were at the point of no return. Just how many chances could one man give me? I was turfed out once more, and this time I believed it was for good. In an act of desperation I told Kevin I'd had an abortion, an evil and wicked lie, which he fortunately saw through very easily. As well as my 'attempted' overdose, months earlier I had threatened to kill myself and Kai during a phone call to Kevin, so he was well versed in my devious cries for help by now.

Cheryl had gone to work arranging some high profile TV appearances. In a bid to aid my recovery, more than anything, she believed by putting me firmly in the spotlight it would be even harder for me to use. Fat chance! But there was at least some money coming in from various bits and pieces Cheryl had arranged, and enough for me to put a deposit and couple of months rent down on a flat on the Limehouse Link in the Docklands area of east London.

Having my own apartment again was great...the TV appearances Cheryl had lined up not so appealing. Not when my cocaine intake was still the worst it had ever been. It didn't come more high profile than an exclusive chat on ITV with Martin Bashir, infamous for his warts and all interviews with the likes of Princess Diana and

Michael Jackson. Cheryl had set this up as another part of her masterplan, but it was tell-all in name only. I was still using, and blagging that I wasn't on national TV, but I was at least fairly convincing for this interview. I told the world I was clean and sober, when I was anything but. Thank God we hadn't announced I was pregnant just yet.

Six weeks later, and there was no hiding my issues when I famously made a complete fool of myself on the aptly-named Channel 4 show, *The Priory*. Again Kevin stood by me, but I now know there was a general consensus among my inner circle that I needed to hit rock bottom, and that my rock bottom would inevitably be about as low as it got. That particular TV appearance is legendary in its own right, and for all the wrong reasons. As usual, I had been taking cocaine all afternoon. Kevin was heartbroken when he saw me bumbling around that sofa with Jamie Theakston and Zoe Ball. I could hardly stand up as I walked in and unable to pronounce Beechy's name.

Back at the flat on The Limehouse Link later that night I was aware I'd fucked up massively, but also numb through my extensive cocaine use. I was all over the papers again, but as always, if I was still able to keep taking gear, then I tried my best to block out any memory of it. Cheryl, who is sadly no longer with us after a battle with cancer, was still fairly new to all my dramas. After successfully getting husband Michael through treatment and helping to deal with his own dark times she believed she was the woman for the job. By now she had hooked me up with therapist Beechy Colclough. As well as Elton John, he had famously treated Michael Jackson and became a TV personality in his own right. Beechy would be instrumental in finding me the treatment I so desperately needed.

It broke Kevin's heart if he came to see me at the flat. I was showing with his baby and still high as a kite. Kevin's mum told him that she worked out I was pregnant, just by the way I looked on the Bashir interview, before he even had a chance to tell her. When in February Kevin's mum passed away, I told him in a text "she's fucking dead, get over it". What a bitch, what a nasty piece of work I had become. How could I be so heartless? Soon after those callous comments Kevin relapsed with cocaine - understandably given the circumstances. My nonchalant attitude to such a pivotal moment in his life was hard to take, even though he knew it was the drugs talking. On top of all that, I was in such a bad way that he thought I was about to die with his unborn child. He was also worried that if I didn't make it he would then have nothing to do with Kai, as he had no legal rights. It was enough to turn anybody to drugs, but that was and is his only relapse.

Kevin soon got himself back on the straight and narrow again, and as distant as our relationship had been over the last few months we could, at least, understand and appreciate each other's personal battles. When you're clean and you've lost that kind of destructive lifestyle, you're left with yourself. When you give up one addiction, you always replace it with another. Kevin's addiction became me. Mine was still myself.

Up until then, Kevin's mum was the only person who understood him. I was certainly in no condition to understand him fully. Kevin had and has a fractured relationship with his dad, and I think deep down Kevin still holds a huge amount of resentment towards me because of how inappropriate and inconsiderate I was around the time of his mum's death, but despite that he still stood by me. Kevin never really got a chance to grieve his mum's passing because he was immediately forced to turn his attention to me. I was meant to be clean when I did the Bashir interview, and I may have been for a day or two, but I too relapsed massively around the time of Kevin's mum's death, probably reassuring myself that if he had, then I definitely could.

I was so self-obsessed and I just wasn't there for him. My priority was always cocaine. At my flat at The Highway I had a stash of coke hidden away in a wardrobe. As per the Bashir interview, and Cheryl's PR stance since *The Priory* TV show debacle, I was meant to be in the middle of a strict two week detox ahead of my planned treatment, which Beechy was organising at the Cottonwood Tuscon treatment centre in Arizona.

The party line was that I was behaving, but that was anything but the truth. I still had access to, and was using, cocaine. I had enough gear for now, but not enough of Kevin's attention. He hadn't been to see me for a few days, and I was desperate for him to visit. I craved his attention as much as cocaine. I told my friend Vanessa that I would kill myself if he didn't show up soon.

In the past I have painted a picture of painfully going through the cold turkey I needed to endure to be clean enough to fly. Those were the stipulations in place, and it was hugely painful, but mainly because I was still using coke right up until I got on the actual plane. By the time I did stagger through the departure lounge I was a physical and emotional wreck, literally with weeks to live. However I looked at it, I would be in pain...if I kept using or stopped.

Badgering Vanessa had the desired affect. She begged Kevin on the phone to come over, assuring him that I wanted to do the treatment. He was at the end of his tether, growing increasingly tired of jumping when I said so. He was not long clean himself and trying to restructure his business and reeducate the people around him...which wasn't easy. Kevin keeping in contact with me was a necessary evil, and at least a distraction from his business affairs.

Kevin was still getting invited to sort out the various scrapes that some of his cohorts found themselves in, despite being sober, clean and not, as they say in the business "tooled up". The new Kevin foolishly went to someone's house thinking he could sort something out in a more diplomatic way, and received another big wake-up call. A Range Rover pulled up outside the property, and Kevin looked around the room and saw the whole thing for what it was. He was the only one not sniffing or 'holding'. It suddenly dawned on him how ridiculous it all was...these tooled-up, charged-up guys, slowly getting off their heads on coke, while they waited for a tear-up. Kevin went outside to front the guys in the 'Range' and someone must have been looking down on him, because the car slowly reversed out of the driveway, and drove off. It seemed that Kevin's presence there alone carried enough weight on that occasion. However, he no longer wanted that presence, let alone to know it still had the desired affect.

When Kevin did make it round to see me, he was shocked. Seeing me still coked up, just like all his old henchmen, made the whole thing even more poignant to him. Was he the only sane person around here? Of course, I was pregnant too. Kevin had seen me in some bad states before, but this topped the lot. He said it was the worst he'd ever seen me, and that must have been saying something. I had been prescribed special detox medication, to help bring me off the coke, but I was taking that and loads of coke as well, after consistently managing to smuggle more into the flat since I had moved in.

I was showing heavily, and to make matters worse Kai had chicken pox, which is such a dangerous thing to be around when you're pregnant. My mood was changing by the second, like I was possessed, but the actress in me meant I still sounded like I wanted to do the treatment. I managed to convince Kevin, and was desperate for him to stay the night with me. Kevin was having none of it. Blunt and cold, he told me: "Make no mistake. This isn't us getting back together. This is you going into treatment. I'm going home." Not what I wanted to hear. I went mental, picked up a portable TV and threw it at Kevin. It just missed, and crashed against the wall behind him. A security guard Cheryl had employed to keep an eye on me, came in and broke things up, and Kevin left.

Cheryl thought she could manage me, but she couldn't. Nobody could for any long period of time. She employed the same security that looked after Michael Barrymore when he was ill. Of course, Cheryl's heart was in the right place, but in the short time he had known me Kevin had heard and seen it all before. He had spent thousands of pounds on various therapies, treatments and rehabs for me by now, and he was being told that this time was for real.

As much as Kevin and I were apart at that time, I think Cheryl tried to cut Kevin out of things too. She tried her best to manage me, and I can understand why she wanted to have a free run at it. Eventually she had to throw the towel in and call Kevin to admit it was beyond her team.

Like many people, including myself, Cheryl didn't know all the facts or what she was dealing with. I was probably badmouthing Kevin to her as well which wouldn't have helped, but in reality then, and always, Kevin is the person who can handle me best.

It was so hard for him to get a handle on the desperate sight that greeted him as he drove back along The Highway in the pouring rain. He could just about make out someone standing in the middle of the road, waving their arms in the air manically. It was me, dressed in just a T-Shirt and a pair of knickers, looking like the woman in the film The Ring. I had given my guard the slip, climbed out of a window at the back of the flat and staggered through on-coming traffic onto the central reservation. Kevin screeched to a halt in the middle of the road, leapt out, and grabbed me as I stumbled in between speeding cars. He dragged me across to the other side of the road and handed me back to the minder. He couldn't take me back himself, he knew he'd never get out of that flat and that tough love was the only way forward now...the toughest he'd dished out yet. He rang Cheryl on her mobile and told her: "Book her into that clinic in Arizona now...get her over there now!"

DANNIELLA WESTBROOK

6

NOW OR NEVER

The sight of me half-naked, pranged, pregnant and drenched, dragged kicking and screaming from the middle of a dual-carriageway by a security guard was Kevin's last image of me before I headed to Arizona. You could say it was a fitting end to my crippling and all-consuming drug addiction. But you couldn't blame him for thinking I had a cat in hell's chance of getting clean.

Within 48 hours I was at Cottonwood, the treatment centre that would save my life. I had been told that a one-way ticket to the States had been booked for me...no return flights planned any time soon. In fact, given my reputation and condition, Virgin were the only airline who would take me. I'm told someone apparently got a message to Richard Branson and he OKd it. That was amazing of him, but he does have a history of helping people with addictions over the years, like he did Boy George when he was signed to Virgin Records.

My time at the Cottonwood Tucson in Phoenix, Arizona, was my very own last chance saloon, just like it was the final throw of the dice for Paul Gascoigne in 2013 when he also headed to Arizona for treatment, at a clinic called The Meadows. Both Cottonwood and The

Meadows regularly appear in lists for the Top 10 rehab centers in the world, so there must be something about the fresh mountain air out there. However, unlike Gazza, I didn't need the likes of Chris Evans, Gary Lineker, Piers Morgan and Ronnie Irani to have a whip-round for my rehab costs. It has been reported that these high profile friends raised a six-figure sum for his initial six weeks of treatment. *The Sun* also ran an appeal for donations, while The Football Association and the England Footballer's Foundation both donated £20,000 each. Like Gazza, I didn't have the money for my treatment either - roughly £20,000 back then for my six week stay - but there was only one man footing the bill...and, yes, his name was Kevin. It's yet another example of how both spoilt and lucky I was to have him.

Cottonwood was where I first had any dealings with God, the first time I experienced anything vaguely spiritual. As I sat outside at the treatment centre in the early hours one night, looking up at the amazing Phoenix skyline, famed for its alleged paranormal sightings, I tried to talk to God. I asked him, if he was up there and listening, to prove it. I said: "If you're up there and have a plan for me, you need to show me, because I'm ready for your help. I can't do this on my own. My way doesn't work. I need to live. I want you in my life, and if you'll take me, then I'm ready."

I don't know where that came from, or why it happened, and I didn't think much more about it for many years, but as I sat there for several more hours and watched the sun come up, the sunrise created these amazing colours. Then I went inside, and got on with my chores at the centre, cleaning up the dorm everyone shared, the usual bits and pieces we were required to do. Despite having no sleep I felt lighter, like I possessed a new inner strength or some kind of new-found faith in myself. For the first time I could see a plan that I would have this baby, that I could save my relationship and get my son back...and all finally without drugs.

Kevin says when I entered Cottonwood, he not only had little hope this latest bout of rehab would help, he had no intentions of getting back with me either. I was pregnant with his child, of course, but in his mind he had pretty much washed his hands of me, on a relationship level, at the very least.

But I was slowly on the mend. After my successful stint in Arizona, I went to Florida for after-treatment for a couple of weeks, and gradually started to get some clarity back in my life. I literally felt like a new person. I went in completely psychotic, and although I was still extremely vulnerable when I came out, for the first time after any treatment I was ready for a fresh start. It was also the first time I gave a shit about the hole in my nose.

The more Kevin and I talked on the phone the more he could see I really did mean business, and the more he says he fell in love with the new me. I was just relieved there was someone, underneath, to fall in love with.

When I returned to the UK, we took it one day at a time, but we did start seeing each other. It was like dating again for the first time. Like two people courting and sounding each other out...and all while I was pregnant with our child. It was hardly conventional, but then we hadn't ever done normal. We both look back at this time as a beautiful and special moment in our lives.

I moved in with Kevin at his new house in Bexleyheath, yet another change of scenery, but this time more than any, a much-needed fresh start. However, there was one vital piece of the jigsaw missing. While I was in Arizona, social services had placed Kai with his dad, and he clearly wasn't going to come back to me immediately on my return. It was so hard. Several times, as I drove through Bermondsey, I saw Kai with his dad Robert, but as I had started to fight for custody again, and because of the court order, I wasn't even allowed to wave at him, let alone have a quick chat or a hug. Fortunately now, I did know there was a bigger picture. Kevin and I worked hard on providing the sort of family stability needed to convince social services it was safe for Kai to return. I knew it wouldn't be a formality, not with my history and the recent circumstances, but at least there was a chance of stability now.

Before any confirmed news of Kai's return, on September 5, 2001...our very own miracle, Jodie B, was born. Kai was a miracle himself, given that I used all the way through and during the pregnancy, but, in her own way, Jodie's health was just as much of a blessing, given how ravaged my body was when she was conceived and how easily I could have died during the rest of that nine-month term. For once Kevin and I joined forces, devoting our whole time to Jodie B and our bid to get Kai back. I was defiant I'd stay clean and sober, so there was no booze either. Kevin could see how determined I was and, in total, I think he took a whole year off work. He felt he needed to be with me constantly, because he feared any bad news about Kai or difficulties coping with a new baby could set me back. But thank God Kai did return, the day before his fifth birthday, November 22, 2001. Another truly momentous moment in my life.

I can now look back fondly at the few months after leaving Cottonwood, but in reality I was in a precarious situation. After proving myself to Kevin I had embarked on four of the most stressful things anyone can go through in life...battling for custody of my child through the courts, having another baby, moving house and (hopefully) finally getting married. Those around me had seen me clean for a couple of weeks at a time on several occasions, but it never lasted, and never looked like lasting. Now cleaner than ever I did sense that everyone was holding their breaths, waiting for me to slip up again. Hoping I wouldn't, but certain I would.

And I couldn't blame anyone for having extreme doubts. When I finally got home to the UK, after my convalescing period in Florida, I didn't expect anyone to believe this time would be the one...why would they? It was pointless even saying that I was definitely going to change, they'd heard all that bullshit before, and then found within a couple of weeks I'm lying or stealing off them again. I knew action would mean so much more now than words. When, after a period of time, people could see that I wasn't back to my old ways again, that I had changed and wasn't trying to weave my black magic any more, then they could finally stop walking on eggshells and relax a little.

With our family finally complete and both of us clean and sober, getting married seemed the logical progression. Kevin had, of course, proposed to me when we first met two years earlier.

We'd booked the Conran Hotel at Chelsea Harbour for the wedding and reception, the day after Boxing Day. We must have booked out most rooms in that hotel. There was a sit down meal for 250 people, with a further 200 people invited in the evening.

On the surface it was all smiles. We were doing an OK Magazine shoot and life couldn't be better. However, our pink cloud moment came to an abrupt halt in the run up to the big day when all of Kevin's family declined their invitations to the wedding. The Jenkins' snub was hardly surprising considering the contempt Kevin's dad had for me. When his wife only had weeks to live I was constantly ringing down the family phone demanding to speak to Kevin. Shouting the odds at such a delicate time was so inappropriate.

When Kevin's mum did pass away, he spent as much time with his dad as possible, trying to build bridges. He took him to America on holiday and tried to bond with him. He is the youngest of three children, and was always seen as a rebel because of the various 'career' paths he has taken over the years. Barry Jenkins, OBE, is big in the British film industry, and owned ABC Cinemas at one point. Kevin went to see him just before Jodie B was born and told him we were getting married. Barry was defiant, telling him: "You can bring the baby and Jordan to this house, but not her."

It was a kick in the bollocks for Kevin. A crushing blow. But we weren't shocked when his dad refused to come to the wedding, or when the rest of the family followed suit. We were, of course, disappointed.

It wasn't like a slow process of excluding me from the family. I had never been popular in the Jenkins household. When Kevin and I started dating a couple of years earlier, he was still a massive part of his family. It was expected that he had Sunday lunch at the family home every week, whatever he was up to the night before, or that morning! He would never take me, though. There were always impressionable teenagers present so turning up with the country's best-known cocaine addict was clearly not a good look.

In his family's eyes, Kevin had only ever been associated with drama - mine and his - so I think it's comfortable for the Jenkins to leave us in the past. It was probably with a huge sigh of relief that they could. Kevin's dad stood his ground, and so did Kevin. The other thing they did have in common was that they had both lost the woman they had been the closest to in their lives. Kevin had effectively chosen me over his family. It was another massive sacrifice and one, at times over the years, I know I should have appreciated more. Kevin says the wedding snub was like all of his family died in a plane crash, and to this day he has rarely spoken to any of them since. His cousin Alan, bless him, has always been around...through the good and bad times, and has never asked for anything from us.

We were so happy to be getting married, but it was also a shit time for all of us. Kevin desperately wanted his family to finally accept me...the new me, and I felt terribly guilty at the pain and suffering I had caused the Jenkins.

And it was a new me. But that's when the hard work begins. You get well, and expect everyone to applaud, but they don't. They're still hurt at all the pain you have caused them over the years. As much as nobody could believe it, or maybe wanted to believe it, things had changed. We had changed. It's so sad because when Jodie B was born and we got married, Kevin was no longer this angry underworld-type character, and I was not the drugged-up cokehead everyone had become accustomed to. But I can't blame them. I actually make Kevin's dad right. If ever Kai has a girlfriend, who is ringing up, off her tree, making no sense, while one of our family is seriously ill, then I probably won't speak to her again either.

7

MIND YOUR MANORS

After the highs and lows of the wedding, as a family, we cherished having our beautiful baby Jodie B in our lives, and Kai back where he belonged. So the slow process of being off cocaine forever began for me. In Cottonwood I was taught that your worst day off drugs is better than your best day on drugs. That being off drugs doesn't have to be a life sentence. That you don't have to wear that for the rest of your life, although that's debatable if you've played out your entire adult life in the tabloids, like me.

They do stress, however, that if you have a problem finding what they call your 'happy place' after two years, then you need to seek medical help. Like you have radiotherapy when you have cancer, then you may need medicine to cope with being free of drugs. This is something I would eventually appreciate when I finally accepted I was on the bipolar spectrum. It's hard for an addict to accept that any form of medication on a regular basis is the way forward, but it is recommended in many cases.

It was clear I had a lot of hard work ahead of me, and it is a lot to take in, especially in a new relationship with a newborn child.

On the surface, it appeared that life couldn't be any better, but I still had huge nagging doubts about my past. There were deep-rooted issues about certain situations I had found myself in over the years, the depths I had sunk, the trauma I had suffered, and one particular event I couldn't even tell Kevin about. It would and will continue to haunt me for the rest of my life. Now was certainly not the time to address it, and so this new positive phase of our relationship and lives continued. I enjoyed it the best I could, at least confident I was in the best place possible to deal with any new issues or dramas that came our way.

Like any honeymoon period in a relationship, Kevin and I started to make plans. He had this romantic idea that he wanted to open a restaurant in Great Portland Street, just down the road from the hospital where our baby daughter was born, and we fittingly planned to call it Jodie B Brasserie. Kevin hadn't been at Premier much since I'd come back from Arizona and Florida. There had been Jodie B's birth, and prior to that he'd spent long periods of time either getting treatment of his own, being with his mother for those last few months or digging me out of yet another hole. He reckons in total he hadn't been involved in the business on a day-to-day basis for the best part of 18 months.

We were quite a way down the line with the restaurant. The site was identified and negotiations were at an advanced stage. Kevin had worked out that a five figure sum would be needed each week from the Premier coffers to get it up and running, and was number-crunching like mad to see if we could make it happen. One of Gordon Ramsay's sommeliers was going to come and work for us. We had chosen fixtures and fittings, and even started to pick out some crockery. Kevin suggested we book a place in Cannes for a few weeks so he could work on some more ideas for the restaurant. My recovery period was still raw, and it was still a massive case of one day at a time, so spending more time away from central London made sense.

Straight and sober, I could now focus on purchasing much more elaborate things than bags of white powder, so a trip to the South of France and a stint checking out all the boutiques there was fine with me, thank you very much. However, soon after we arrived, it all went tits up. Kevin was going through the figures for the restaurant. When he dug deeper he realised that, while he hadn't been around, Premier had virtually been run into the ground, and was on the verge of going under.

So that was the end of our stay in Cannes, and the last I would see of Kevin properly for some time. When we returned to the UK, the company somehow owed a total of £1.8m. Something had clearly gone very badly wrong. Kevin had taken his eye off the ball to be with his mum, and to try and save me, and us. It was some sacrifice, but totally understandable where his mum was concerned.

Kevin worked six days a week, 18 hours a day, for the best part of two years to turn things around and get the company back on its feet. He almost relished the challenge, but I knew it would take so much out of him, and I immediately feared for his health and our relationship. But he did gradually pull Premier back from the brink. Certain people who shall remain nameless were demoted, or accepted lesser positions for their part in the fiasco, but ultimately nobody was sacked. The company had been saved, but Kevin was a wreck. He headed straight back to The Priory for an urgent consultation, where the staff wanted to admit him, and sedate him. However, he had promised us a family holiday to Portugal, and ever the man of his word, went against doctor's orders and we headed to the Algarve. But Kevin's head was so muddled still. One day, by the pool at our villa, he was literally melting in front of our eyes. At one point he forgot mine and the kid's names. When we got back to the UK I let him rest at home, and he was diagnosed with glandular fever, probably brought on by being so run down.

Kevin's health improved over the next few weeks, and he would need his wits about him because, with the help of my new favourite website - *www.primelocation.com* - I had located my dream house! Now, my new addiction was badgering Kevin to buy this luxury pile for us. House hunting is like porn to me. I love looking at new properties, and I live for moving houses. I love all the TV shows. Grand Designs is right up there, but my personal favourite is Country House Rescue. I frickin' love that one. I love old properties, with a history. I missed that when we lived in LA, so I'd go to Long Beach for something a bit more retro.

Right now we were living in a five bed house in a village in Kent called Hartley but I had grand designs of my own. I came across Gads Hill House, situated in a nearby village called Higham, just down the road from Gads Hill Place, famously the country retreat of Charles Dickens. If I couldn't play restaurants, then I was now intent on playing country manors.

Gads Hill House was a seven-bedroomed house built in 1834 and, on first inspection, it didn't look like a lot had been done to it since. I took Kevin to see it, and he reckons it was one of the spookiest experiences of his life. There were literally ghosts all over that place, but that wasn't going to put me off. I hounded Kevin for a full year, begging him to buy the house, arguing that it was just around the corner from the school where we were sending the kids, and eventually wore him down. So much so that he sold a document storage business he had in Bermondsey to help fund the purchase.

In December 2002, for just shy of a million pounds 'we' bought Gads Hill House...referred to in my last book briefly as "a lovely house". To say there was loads that needed doing to this place is in an understatement, and Kevin and I both wanted it restored from top to bottom, all three floors of it. We converted the cellars into a self-contained apartment. We knocked two of the bedrooms through to make one massive one for ourselves. We added a 2,000 square feet indoor pool and gym annexe, complete with crosstrainer, treadmill, free weights area and a punch bag.

The swimming pool itself showed how gluttonous we had become. We had it shipped over in one piece from Holland. It came complete with a swim against wave machine feature and we installed three waterfalls at the back. A glass wall separated the pool and the gym so we could keep and eye on the kids, and a state-of-the-art fingerprint entry system was installed so they couldn't gain access without us. There was mood lighting, a remote-controlled retractable cover for the pool, the compulsory wicker furniture and a massive flat screen TV on the wall so I could watch Jeremy Kyle or *The Wright Stuff* while I was training in the mornings.

We had lived in two nice houses before this, and always had a pool, both in Bexleyheath and Longfield, but the sheer opulence of what we were creating here was off the scale. Inside there was a massive play room for the kids and a 40ft dining room. Outside in our expansive six acres of grounds we had a quad track laid out, and even a golf hole, despite the fact neither of us have ever played golf, and had no plans to. It was ridiculous, but I just couldn't see it at the time.

There was one big issue to overcome, though, and that was the spooks that seemingly haunted this huge house. We were only the fourth family to live there since the early 1800s. A tunnel from the main house down to the local church was on the deeds, but we never knew why or found it. Each of us during our time there saw the same guy floating about the place. And a woman...she would pop up from time to time too. We kind of got used to it in the end. However, some of the builders' tools wouldn't work there. They'd go and work on other sites just down the road, plug them in and they'd be fine, then come back to our's and they wouldn't work. That held things up on quite a few occasions. It was bizarre. The builders were in for a total of 18 months, and we spent a lot of time living in the dining room, while various rooms were being done.

Mum and her boyfriend Eddie bought one of the workhouse cottages on our estate, and while that was being done up they stayed in the apartment within the house, which was great because they could keep an eye on things when we weren't around. We also employed Eddie as a gardener and general handyman who helped maintain the grounds.

And so we kept spending. I was way out of control, but had no idea. We bought a vintage chandelier from an old chateau in France...getting that over was fun, a potential Only Fools & Horses turn out. We had a grand piano installed at one end of the dining room, despite the fact nobody played. I had the whole house painted in cream and decked out in marble...Chanel colours, and very Chigwell. Original Herringbone flooring was laid throughout. When I think back now, we were like lottery winners and it was all quite vulgar. Nobody had used the grounds that much before and we were racing round the place in quad bikes like chavs whose numbers had just come up. We had Bentleys, Ferraris and Porsches parked outside the front, and Kai's bedroom was decked out in Gucci wallpaper.

We had a house full most Sundays. Loads of friends would come over with their kids, to use the pool. We were happy to entertain and we wanted other people to enjoy Gads.

Kevin paid his staff well. He would usually hold his board meetings at home, because it was central for everyone, but when the staff pulled in and saw all the cars, the indoor pool and the gym I worried they would slowly start to hate us. Kevin was always generous with his money and paid people, and looked after them, very well. He collected a lot of hangers-on along the way, and I think money is even worse than fame for that.

Despite all the extravagance, I'd like to think we were still ourselves, just in a bigger house. You still got offered a cup of tea on arrival, whoever you were. Personally, I don't think a working class family should live in a house like that. We were clearly well out of our league. It's not meant for people like us. You think you're moving up the ladder, but I believe people with old money will always appreciate and respect this kind of property much more. I must have thought I was a footballers' wife or something, and I was clearly acting like one. In reality I was like Del Boy when he finally became a millionaire. It just wasn't all it was cracked up to be. I would regularly cry myself to sleep, or hide myself away in our bedroom. Some days I just couldn't face what we had created.

(clockwise) ✧ Our girl, Jodie ✧ With my brother Jay, aka 'Sarge' ✧ In Spain with Jodie ✧ A rad shot from Kai's photoshoot with JamDeluxe ✧ Family time in Las Vegas ✧ Kevin's eldest Jordan - "one of my own" - with Jodie and I ✧ My favourite tattoo, by Miss Cookie...says it all for me!

(clockwise) ✧A big hug with 'The Osbournes'... Sharon and Ozzy... love these guys! ✧ With Heather Mills at Dancing On Ice ✧ One for the haters...me and my TOWIE mate Harry Derbidge ✧ Skating with Matt Gonzalez, live on Dancing On Ice

(clockwise) ✧ With our darling godson Enzo Luciano ✧ Mel, me, Lili and Lisa, out for dinner in Huntington Beach ✧ Lunch in Santa Monica with our old buddy 'Grecs' ✧ With my 'homie' Christy Haizlip

(clockwise) ✧ Pampered at my cover photoshoot by the marvellous Jam Deluxe boys, JaySam and Michael, both also pictured with me below.

◇ Me and Jodie and (inset) Kai at my book launch

8
CHECK MATE

Much of the press I have received over the years has hardly been anything to brag about. However, I've obviously had my fair share of column inches. A friend of mine reckons to be the subject of one iconic photograph in your lifetime is momentous enough, but to be in another, is about as good as it gets.

The harrowing image in the first photograph is anything but 'momentous', but I guess it's true that the gaping nose shot is fairly iconic...if not pathetic. Unlike that photo, the second in question wasn't as literal as it seemed. It not only typified what my life had become, but it was also hailed as being responsible for the birth of the 'chav'...and, it was claimed, a PR disaster for one of the UK's oldest fashion houses. I'm talking about, of course, the legendary Burberry photograph, which I can now reveal was stunted up with a member of the paparazzi because, in his words, it was a "slow day".

I pitched up in New Bond Street in January, 2003 and was heading to Burberry anyway, when I bumped into a 'pap' I knew. He said it was really quiet and suggested we do something. I was wearing the kilt in the famous Burberry check anyway, and was carrying a bag too, so I went inside the store and spoke to the assistant about the baby buggy. I'd had my eye on it for a while, and so splashed out £1,500 on that, and bought Jodie B, who was with me, a matching kilt. I put that on her inside the shop and then came out with her in the buggy. Lights, camera, action and, hey presto, we had our shot. I even made sure that I took Jodie out of the buggy because otherwise you wouldn't have been able to see she was wearing the kilt too. I said to the pap that we could share any proceeds from the picture, but I let him keep it all in the end. It was actually just nice to work with a pap for a day.

The photograph spread like wildfire, and was everywhere the next day and for the following week. Burberry's image took a battering and sales, and their share price, were said to have dipped over the following months..

Over the years many have had their own take on the picture and chaos we had unwittingly caused at Burberry. The Guardian ran an article suggesting that there is one image throughout the history of Burberry that first springs to mind. It said I was: "*clad top to toe in Burberry check*" and that Jodie was: "*dressed to match, as if she rolled in it like a pig in muck.* The article went on to claim that the Burberry check had become the ultimate symbol of: "*nouveau rich naff.*"

I am also a notable entry in the Burberry section of online fashion bible *Voguepedia.* The timeline dates back to 1856 when Thomas Burberry, a 21-year-old English draper's assistant opens an outfitters shop in Basingstoke. It goes on to chart the entire history of the label throughout the 20th Century, and I pop up at the start of 2003:-

"The (Daniella Westbrook) image sparks widespread media ridicule; and the design becomes known as "chav check".

Newspapers ran reports of pubs banning drinkers wearing the brand, and, a year later, Burberry apparently stopped making baseball caps in their famous check. The fact that media and fashion commentators have taken the whole thing so seriously and the picture itself continues to cause such interest, always amazes me.

I thought the 'chav' fall-out was all quite fitting, because I believe it's the working classes who keep a lot of those designer brands going...who save up their hard-earned cash to go and shop at Gucci or Tiffany or wherever. I did quite well out of the whole Burberry-gate thing, through various interviews in the papers and on TV about the chav phenomenon. Just like the nose photo, the Burberry one is shown again and again. Whenever Burberry is in the spotlight, if it's had a good year or a bad year, they wheel out the picture, and, of course, it always makes me chuckle, knowing exactly how it all came about.

However, the money we spent in that period was no laughing matter. In fact, it was obscene. I would spend £400 at a time on Juicy Couture tracksuits or £600 on a Stone Island jacket for Kai, when he was seven, and he always wore Prada shoes for school. The Gucci bits I bought for Jodie were beautiful, but ridiculous... £120 for some house slippers? I once paid £85 for a Gucci milk bottle holder for Jodie when she was a baby, and even bought a nappy changing bag for three times that amount, although she has since used that as a school bag, so we did get our money's worth out of that one...sort of.

We had Versace ashtrays at home and always bought the cleaner a gift from Louis Vuitton at Christmas. Our spending was off the hook. Kevin bought his minder Luc a Rolex the first Christmas I was with him, and he had the cheek to complain it was the wrong one. Kev took him to New Bond Street the next day to change it, and paid an extra three grand for the one he did want. I remember joking: "I thought I was the spoilt brat around here." Luc even bought Versace ashtrays for his three-bed semi.

I suppose we thought buying people lovely things would make them happy, but we found out that wasn't always the case. If anything, I think some people may have resented us even more.

Then there were the cars. Kevin had a Ferrari and a Bentley Flying Spur. During one period I had a Hummer H3, a Range Rover Sport and a Porsche 911 Carrera 4S, all at the same time. All these cars where leased through Premier, so we didn't notice the cost...well, I certainly didn't anyway. Kevin bought me a Mercedes SL350 one day, and was so excited to hand me the keys. I had a

Jaguar XKR at the time and he unveiled this new 'Merc' to me on the huge driveway at Gads one morning. I slowly walked around it and, after a pause, said "Hmmm?...I wanted the SL55 AMG." Kevin was furious, called me a "spoilt bitch" and told the guy who had just dropped it off to take it straight back. Kevin kept it stored at the Premier offices for a good three months after that before he would let me drive it.

These days our spending habits are a million miles away from all that. Like a lot of women, I'm a big fan of Primark. Back then I loved Chloe, and in the '90s John Richmond in Covent Garden or loads of labels at Jones in Floral Street. Now, you're more likely to find me in Top Shop or Next. I've always liked the classic look of Joseph and Nicole Farhi, which is obviously a bit more expensive, but I also love my sweats and Adidas Originals or Nike trainers, big hoodies and streetwear brands like Stussy.

I recently bagged up 16 black sacks of designer clothes, and took them to a local charity shop, the St Clare's Hospice. I know the staff there well and the proceeds go to a good cause. I kept a few bits back for Jodie, some stuff that she might find useful in a few years time, but I'll be a pensioner by the time some of the other bits come back around, Vivienne Westwood and Dolce & Gabbana coats for instance, which had long had their time.

I'm also pretty-much over cosmetic surgery, although I wouldn't totally rule out the odd nip and tuck in the future. I've had a whole host of procedures over the years, not least several operations to fix my nose. Like many women in the entertainment business I wanted to boost my bust size. I guess its the nature of the beast when, like me, you're consistently being offered glamour shoots with various lads mags and tabloid newspapers. I'm not the first soap star to do the lads mags and I certainly won't be the last.

On the face of it four boob jobs is excessive, but I have had various problems with the type of enhancements used along the way. For my first operation in the mid '90s I had silicone and it took me from my natural breast size of 32B to a 32C. In February 1998 one of the implants was ruptured in a car accident I was involved in and so a second op at the end of the '90s took me to a 34D. This time I went down the natural route and had soya implants. This means you can see behind the breast wall...the chest plate. I've also always made sure with any boob job I've had, that the implant goes under the muscle, so it never sits on the top. In my opinion, that's when they can start looking strange.

A third operation in 2002 was excessive. My soya implants had started to leak and obsessed with Pamela Anderson I went huge, up to a 34EE. This time they were ma-hoosive...but not as massive as I had wanted. My surgeon Mr Frame was talking to Kevin behind my back, and they agreed to limit this op to 'EE'. I wanted them to be 'FF' or 'GG' or something stupid. Kevin says from a bloke's perspective they were simply so big and fake they were a complete turn-off to him anyway. I called them Phil and Grant, after my on-screen brothers, as they reminded me of Ross and Steve's bald heads. Sorry boys. They did look weird and my nipples were all over the place. Kevin said there was one looking up at the ceiling, and the other looking out of the window. And he was right...there was one looking at you and one looking for you.

My back was under so much strain. I was way too heavy up top and I eventually had the implants taken out because they had simply become too painful. I had to wait two or three months before I had the replacements inserted, but in 2005 I did just that, and went down a few sizes to a 34DD. That was thankfully my last boob job and I'm so happy where I am with them now.

I was also pleased to leave glamour modelling behind. My first lads mag shoot with Loaded Magazine in 1996 saw me on the cover, in a baby doll lingerie set, with a Chupa Chup lollipop in my mouth and the headline 'SUCK ON THIS'. Classy stuff. Back then, I was 23, not yet pregnant and happy for any cash I could get my hands on, as my coke habit continued to spiral out of control. In those days a Loaded cover was pretty prestigious. I had followed the likes of Elle MacPherson, Uma Thurman and Kylie Minogue, and stars like Cindy Crawford, Cameron Diaz, Catherine Zeta Jones, Britney Spears, Angelina Jolie and my hero Pamela Anderson, would all grace the Loaded cover over the next few years too, so I was in good company. That Chupa Chup picture is a well-known shot in its own right, and recently featured in a collection of Loaded's 'all-time sexiest cover girls', but that now seems so '90s and very of its time.

In the first 18 months of being clean, getting married and having my nose done, I started to take a long hard look at myself. Guys would shout at me in the street "Oi, cokehead, get your tits out," and as a mother with two young kids there's probably not much more degrading than that. I had clearly left myself open to such comments, because I had happily posed for plenty of half-naked photo shoots for various publications while using drugs, but also since being clean. In the run-up to getting clean in 2000/01 I would take any old glamour job I could find, particularly those that paid cash up front. Post recovery, my addiction to boob jobs meant I continued for a few years, and I was doing those kinds of shoots right up until my stint on I'm A Celebrity in 2003.

I suddenly had a reality check. I remembered I was an actress not a glamour model. Getting my kit off for the likes of Loaded and Front Magazine was obviously all about self-obsession, trying to fill voids in my life, self-gratification and feeling worthless. It's unfortunately how a lot of girls in that business feel. Kai wasn't a toddler any more, and as I grew older and cleaner I thankfully decided my glamour modelling days were over. I won't rule out a 'looking great at 40' shoot for a woman's magazine or newspaper, though, but only if I put some serious time in at the gym, and maybe even as a way of making sure I do keep up my gym regime.

Botox is another beauty treatment I've dabbled with for quite some time. For years I had Botox injections every two or three months. Eventually the skin on my face was tighter than the kids'. Eventually I couldn't shut my eye lids fully. On one holiday I looked like an action man, with eagle eyes going from side to side as I tried to shield them from the sun. My surgeon, Mr Frame, told me everything that was bad about Botox, but I rarely listened.

I've also done the whole colonic thing, and had lip injections a couple of times after a friend in LA suggested it. I was petrified about having my lips done, but Kevin didn't even notice so I knew I hadn't gone over the top. You do see a lot of horror stories in the papers and I was worried my mouth would blow up like Pete Burns. I stopped the Botox when we moved to LA, because suddenly I wasn't trying to impress anyone. I'd made a conscious decision not to pursue a career in the industry out there. In my mind, I wasn't Danniella Westbrook anymore.

My extensive experience with cosmetic surgery, not least with the multiple operations I had to repair my nemesis, the gaping hole in my nose, made me an ideal candidate to be a presenter on Channel 5's *Cosmetic Surgery Live* special in 2004. I loved doing the show, and working with Vanessa Feltz. She's an absolute legend and a true professional.

I was also well versed in spooks when I was offered a presenting role in TV medium Derek Acorah's special live edition of *Most Haunted* on Living TV in 2003, but the fact that I had a haunted house of my own was pure coincidence. In 2005 I was approached to be part of a new series Derek was fronting called *Ghost Towns*, which was also screened on Living TV. With 19 episodes in total, this job would take me all over the UK, and into 2006, and included three live specials from York. I loved working with Derek, who is a real character, and my co-presenter Angus Purden, as we trawled the country hoping to hear from the dead.

I do believe in the spirit world, but I'm no medium, so we left all that to Derek, who is great at what he does. I have always had an obsession with tarot card readers and psychics. Anything linked to the paranormal...regression or even ouija boards. In fact, before I finally left for Cottonwood for treatment, I had been getting off on doing ouija boards, coked out of my head, which was hardly the best preparation for my latest stint of rehab.

With *Ghost Towns* we started off close to my own haunted house in Kent, in Faversham and Maidstone, and went on to Bedford and Northampton, then further north to Shrewsbury, Stafford, Lincoln, Blackpool and Hull, then across to Oswestry on the Welsh borders and back down south to Canterbury and Lowestoft. We certainly did some miles on that trip. Like *Most Haunted* and *Cosmetic Surgery Live* I enjoyed my stint at presenting, and shows like this helped keep me in the spotlight and active work-wise during a period in my life when, financially, I didn't need to work.

Around this time I turned down a role in ITV drama *Bad Girls*, because I didn't think it was right for me. Parts in the new *Crossroads* and *Footballers Wives* were also put to me, but again I wasn't up for them...maybe I thought I already had the life of a WAG. The West End musical *Chicago* also approached me, and I again declined, although maybe I would be interested in a musical or something on the stage in the future.

I certainly took centre stage when I filmed a fitness DVD, *Danniella's Better Body Workout*, for a Christmas release in 2003. I decided I wanted my friends with me, not a load of dancers who I'd never met before. No disrespect ladies, but that also meant I had a whole selection of shapes and sizes involved, from 8 up to 16. We rehearsed twice a week for a couple of months, and it was great fun, learning everything with the girls.

In that interim period around 2002/03/04, when I was turning down acting work, I enjoyed the presenting side of things. *Ghost Towns* was a demanding job. It wasn't scripted, and apart from the odd bit we needed to learn about each part of the country we were visiting, we could do our own pieces to camera, and I loved that. I guess the basic principle, in the nicest sense, was turning up at someone's house or workplace to try and shit them up a bit.

There were some weird things that happened from job to job. The people we visited had already made their minds up that their place was haunted, so it didn't take that much to convince them. The scenes were filmed in darkness, with infrared cameras, so it was spooky already. I probably shouldn't admit this, but, the odd time, if we were having a slow day, and we were looking at a late cut, I did help things along a little bit. One of my favourite tricks was to have a few pebbles in my pocket, and if things were dragging on, and we needed some action before wrapping up for the day, I did throw a few things on the floor to spice things up. Sorry Derek! Most things I couldn't explain, though. Windows smashing, weird noises and whole host of other ghoulish goings-on.

By now, I had also appeared in ITV's flagship reality show *I'm A Celebrity...Get Me Out Of Here*, and, as I struggled with a debilitating depression I now know was bipolar disorder, I used the famous phrase to get me the hell out of that jungle nine days into my time there. You have to complete eight days before you can get paid, so desperately unhappy in there from day one, and missing the kids like hell, I held on as long as I needed to.

My last book covers the period between 2002 - 2004 in matter of pages, ahead of its release in 2006. It doesn't mention *Ghost Towns*, for personal reasons that will become clear. Back then I didn't (and couldn't) shirk major events in my life, but this time I simply knew I must dig even deeper into everything I've been through.

DANNIELLA WESTBROOK

9

BETRAYAL

I was used to having 100 per cent of Kevin's attention...addicted to it, even. But there had been a another hiccup at Premier. Kevin was having to spend all his time at the office, seven days a week, and when he was home his head was still at Premier. As self-obsessed as ever, I felt fat, frumpy and forgotten. It was early 2005, I hadn't yet been asked to do *Ghost Towns*, and I'd not long had a baby.

Hooked on beauty treatments - tanning, nails and Botox - I had recently booked another boob job. That's when I bumped into Stuart Bilton, an old friend of mine when we were kids. Stuart was Posh Spice's boyfriend, when she met David Beckham. It has been reported that he has since dated a host of well-known actresses. In other words, he had form. Now this chance meeting in our native Loughton meant I was firmly on his radar too.

I'd made this rare trip back to Essex to buy some clothes from a designer kids' shops. Me and Stuart go back to when I was 13 or 14, hanging around that area, and it was genuinely nice to see someone from my past, someone who knew me before *EastEnders*, before I was famous and before drugs.

Stuart was his charming self, and explained he was working for an Italian clothing company in New Bond Street. He said he would arrange for some clothes to be sent to my dresser so we exchanged numbers, and started to text each other. It's no excuse, but I now know I wasn't dealing with classic symptoms of bipolar at all well. Deep-rooted issues with psychosis were also hard to shift and severe bouts of depression would come and go. In fact, I still didn't believe I had bipolar disorder. I did, however, know the difference between right and wrong. When a line is crossed. The texts started getting more flirty but I carried on.

It seemed after getting clean Kevin and I were inseparable. He was always around, rarely at the office, but now had been AWOL for months. We had become more and more detached, the attention I craved and needed suddenly gone. The interest Stuart paid in me filled that void momentarily, but Luc had clocked what was going on. I was in the West End every other day, spending two grand a week at Selfridges, and I'd started to meet up regularly with Stuart. Mostly in New Bond Street, at his office...a couple of times a week. Never for lunch or dinner, but maybe over a coffee at Starbucks. The compliments were always flowing, but so were details of various business ideas he was working on.

Then I crossed another line. I foolishly leant Stuart some money...£2,000 from our joint account. Stupid, I know, but he was an old friend, one of the oldest I still had, and I was sure he would get the cash back to me. It didn't seem a lot of money compared to what I was getting through at the time, so I guess I'd lost touch with reality once more, but I did know I needed get it back, pronto, before Kevin noticed it had gone.

By this point I had decided to use a different phone for contact with Stuart. Nonchalantly, I ordered another handset through the business, but Kevin was soon on to me. And, of course he was. He had sifted through an extortionate itemised phone bill on my original mobile and the same number kept cropping up...and at strange times. Kevin had heard Stuart's name mentioned a few times so asked around for his number. When those digits did come back to him - whaddya know? - it was the same number that had kept cropping up on my bill.

There was nothing sexual about this relationship. It wasn't going anywhere in that respect, but the deceit was obvious, and the money I leant Stuart yet more betrayal. By the time Kevin confronted me my old mate had stopped taking my calls...and we were £2,000 down. I was well and truly snookered. I confessed all, but it was too late. Kevin had made his mind up. And I couldn't blame him, I wouldn't have believed me either. He drove to the house later that night to collect his belongings. Kevin booked himself into the The Marriott Hotel in West India Dock at Canary Wharf...and he wasn't coming back any day soon.

Kevin was gone. I was on my own, albeit with two kids and six Dobermans. We'd had various splits along the way, of course...almost every other month when I was using, but this was a big one, and the first one since we were married. I thought this was definitely it now. Clean and sober, this split hit even harder than any of the others. I'd clearly fucked up massively, and as I sat on the front steps of this huge haunted house, smoking a cigarette, with a Hummer, Porsche and Range Rover parked on the driveway, I had everything and nothing. I hadn't drunk a drop of alcohol since I got clean from cocaine, but I picked up a drink that night. I drove down to the 24hr Asda superstore and bought myself several bottles of wine and some Smirnoff Ices. I had a few drinks here and there over the next week. Not the whole lot in one go. Up until then, because the two always seemed to go hand in hand, I was so frightened that if I drank I'd want to take cocaine again.

Over the years I've been able to drink with the best of them, but I never drank a lot in my early clubbing days, because I always preferred to drive. That sounds a nonsense now, because drug driving is as much a crime as drink driving, but back then technically it wasn't, because the police had no way of testing it. So I would bang away at the coke, drink soft drinks all night, and then jump in the car as and when I needed to get home. In fact, I always liked to be the one driving, so I knew I could get out of any tricky situations quickly. My parents weren't big drinkers, and, in context, I've never considered that I had or have a drink problem. I've stressed to Kai recently: "If you're going to a party and people are drinking, know your limits." I'm always reminding him that he doesn't want to be the kid pictured on Facebook the next day in a pool of vomit.

So as I sat there at Gads, all my demons came back to haunt me once again. I drank every day for a week, not loads so I was obliterated, but enough to make me feel comfortably numb. Then I threw what was left of it away, and was forced to deal with the guilt pangs. I hadn't slipped back into my cocaine hell, but I had put myself in a vulnerable position.

Kevin was again refusing to take my calls, but there was at least some text dialogue which meant the kids were able to go and spend time with him at the hotel, usually with our nanny Sue involved. He still didn't want to see me, or have anything to do with me, and as the days and weeks passed I assumed we weren't going to make it this time.

Then one day...a chink of light. Kevin agreed to meet me with the kids so we could all visit a museum near to his hotel as part of some 'family time' together. Of course, the museum was the last thing on my mind, and I made sure I was dressed to impress when we all met up. Kevin reckons I seduced him that day, but I was his wife, after all, so it was hardly illicit! Whatever the case, it did the trick, and Kevin moved back to Gads Hill House within a couple of days. Things were still raw, of course, with neither of us in the mood to back down.

After weeks of Kevin not wanting to talk to me, now he was back in the house, I was soon back on his case about why he had left. I wouldn't drop it, at a time when I should have just kept my head down. No doubt, another huge slice of 'bipolar bad judgement'! Kevin called my bluff by asking me to take a lie detector test, adamant he still didn't believe I was just texting Bilton. I said to him: "Who do you think you are, Jeremy 'fucking' Kyle?" Kevin reckons it was Beechy who suggested the lie detector, but whoever's idea it was, I was incensed. I flew off the handle at the mere mention of it. I had admitted everything about Bilton. For the last time, we had not been having an affair. I had not lied...not on this occasion.

I ran myself a bath, but the bickering continued in our en-suite, and we were still rowing as I laid there soaking. Kevin was still going on about the lie detector as I stood up and reached out for a towel. I was screaming at him, shouting the odds, calling him every name under the sun, when he suddenly placed his hand across my mouth - in a bid to silence me more than anything - and screamed: "Will you just shut the fuck up? I've only been back 24 hours, and we're back to square one." Kevin's hand held my chin gently for no more than a couple of seconds, but when he let go, I slipped, and fell back into the bath. It was handbags, really, and I wasn't seriously hurt, but I got up to my feet, put on my dressing gown, stormed into the bedroom, picked up the phone and dialed 999.

Halfway through my call to the police, Kevin came into the room and I put the phone down. I hadn't accused him of anything yet, but I had spoken to someone. Kevin picked the phone up himself, knowing that the number would have been logged, with a female sounding distressed cut off halfway through her call. He gave the police our address and invited them round, stressing that it was a heated domestic argument that was now over. Within half an hour, three or four police cars pulled up on the huge driveway at Gads in a blaze of flashing blue lights and sirens. It was all very dramatic, but not enough to trouble my dad. He was sat at the end of the garden, on the lawn mower, with his walkman on, and decided to carry on cutting the grass, rather than come and see what we were up to this time...which, says it all, I guess.

Instead of trying to calm the situation, as we waited for the police to arrive, I had been busy in the bedroom, pinching my arms, and my neck to try and make it look like Kevin had hit me or inflicted some kind of pain. It's hard to think about it looking back, and I get very emotional when I do, because that was the last thing he needed, and clearly very irrational too. Maybe my behaviour, more aggression and poor judgement, was bipolar-related and that caused me to act in such a selfish and irresponsible way.

With the police clearly outside, and now banging on the door, Kevin told me to get a grip and went down to let them in. A number of officers were soon loitering inside our large foyer area and we were quickly separated...Kevin in the master bedroom, and me in one of the spare rooms. I had fortunately calmed down by now and told the police I didn't want to pursue anything. Next door Kevin was being asked a series of questions, along the lines of....

"Do you admit you assaulted your wife?

"No."

"Do you admit you grabbed your wife around the face?

"Yes."

"Well, I'm afraid, that is assault, sir."

"That's a matter of opinion."

That last answer had the potential to get Kevin in all sorts of trouble, and it did! He was forced to take a caution...very reluctantly, I may add...just so we could try and move on. But he did take one. Yet another sacrifice for us.

However, I wasn't out of the woods yet, and neither was our relationship. Kevin was still fuming, and even more so now. The next morning he booked a flight to Orlando, hired a car and drove for days to try and collect his thoughts, leaving me alone once again in this huge house. The whole episode further added to my guilt, and I began to mentally prepare myself for an impending

divorce. Surely the game, and my luxury lifestyle, was up now.

After ten days in Florida, Kevin had calmed down enough for me to fly out there with the kids, and our nanny Sue. She was great and her being there meant we had loads of time together to talk things through. Kevin told me he must be mad, that he felt drunk in my presence, that's how strong his love for me was.

Again, I don't know what I'd done to deserve Kevin's support, and I certainly felt I'd done plenty not to receive any. Instead of coming back to the UK, Kevin suggested we head to Los Angeles so we could escape all the publicity from the article. It was somewhere we'd talked about possibly settling one day, after hearing so much about it from so many people we'd met in the States. It probably wasn't the most responsible thing Kevin could have done, as he'd not long got the company back on its feet again, but I wasn't complaining and so we headed to LA for our latest adventure.

The trip to LA did us the power of good, and we started to bond again. It wasn't easy for Kevin to get past recent episodes in our life, but we'd been through so much already in such a short space of time, and there had been such a stress on the family unit in general, that he was fortunately able to put it into context. He wasn't demanding a lie detector test anymore either. Unbelievably, it wouldn't stop me betraying him again.

Shortly after we got back, Kevin had another massive shock. I hadn't paid any tax since the age of 20, and so there were demands from HMRC for a whopping £250k. We had been back home for a couple of days, and were discussing buying a house in California. We had an office at Gads, and were both sitting at our desks. Kevin was looking for something in the drawer of my desk and found all the tax demands that I had been hiding ever since we moved there. He also discovered loans I'd taken out, and that I'd maxed all my debit and credit cards, huge limits the banks had secured against Premier, without asking him. Within days Kevin had been summonsed to a meeting with our bank manager. Kevin didn't know, but I had the manager's mobile number and was ringing him personally, to get loans, overdrafts and cards topped up, often from Selfridges or Blue Water shopping centre

The grand total on what I owed was £470k which Premier would now have to find or, where the tax bill was concerned, I would be heading to prison. It was another massive hit for the company and, if any of the staff found out, potentially disastrous for morale. It also signalled another huge part of the beginning of the end for Premier, mainly because there was only so much Kevin could take. He was quick explain that in having to find the best part of half a million pounds to bail me out, at 40% tax, it meant the company needed to earn nearer to £750k to pay everything off.

Kevin is sure nobody else would have put up with that sort of shit, that I must have had some kind of spell on him. He lost loads of face at Premier having to take that sort of money out of the business.

If my tax affairs and finances were a horror story, then maybe it was fitting that Channel 5 screened my documentary *Danniella Westbrook: EastEnders, Drugs & My New Nose* on Halloween in October 2005. I had not long had a third and final operation on my nose, in which shark cartilage was used to strengthen it, and this was another chance to get my story across, and followed a previous Channel 4 documentary, *My Nose & Me*.

Like my first book, these documentaries allowed me to get my side of the story over, and were clearly sensational and revolved around shocking images of the hole in my nose. Large parts of my life this far has been like a bad nightmare, but as 2006 played out life on the surface, at least, was about as good as it had ever been for me, and for us as a family.

10
THE BUBBLE BURSTS

A new low in August, 2007. I bought Kevin a Rolex watch for his 40th birthday...with £27,000 of his own money. Shortly after, he says he reached his own personal tipping point. A guy who he had been working on a property deal with had a Ferrari 430FI. This supercar cost £150,000 and after this bloke took him for a spin in it, Kevin was besotted. Luc was assigned to get this car for Kevin, at any cost, and Kevin wasn't about to be put off by an 18 month waiting list. He was adamant and said: "Luc, please just get me the car." And he did...in three days. However, when Kevin got behind the wheel he felt empty. He says his world came crashing down as he drove home - a working class boy sat in another needless trophy car.

Just like Kevin was able to be objective about his own drug addiction, he was hit with the realisation of how extreme our gluttony had become, and this Ferrari typified everything that was wrong. It should have been one of the happiest days of his life, a real standout moment, but it meant nothing to him. Kevin reckons that drive home in the Ferrari was when God first spoke to him. When he pulled into the driveway at Gads I was super excited. He simply slumped out of the car, and walked inside the house without saying a word.

I can't say I was at all surprised. I'd been there loads of times when new cars had turned up, so by now it was hardly a life-changing moment. Kevin ordered a Porsche once, and forgot it was turning up, so we were out when they tried to deliver. It was like Kevin had simply become immune to it all, even though this car was a very special one, and the most expensive and exclusive we'd ever had. The new Ferrari was meant to be something to cheer him up because he was so unhappy, both professionally and personally, with the fall-out of the Bilton row and his police caution still weighing heavy on his mind. But this amazing supercar only made Kevin hate himself and, deep down, resent me more.

Kevin had long called himself 'Cashtill Kev'. Whether it was because of builders at the house, staff meeting there or simply me, he reckons he couldn't walk from the bedroom to the front door without spending money. He was forever saying that he was fed up of being a cash cow, and that the only thing he got out of it was "going to work in a nice car." Now, even the cars weren't making him feel better.

Throughout 2007 Kevin predicted the forthcoming economic crash. He's always been great with figures, able to number crunch the nuts and bolts of the various companies he ran in a matter of hours. If a company was losing money, he could turn it around in weeks. He has always prided himself on that.

Back at Gads, on the morning of September 14, 2008, I was in the gym on the crosstrainer. I always had *Sky News* on to see what was happening in the world and some breaking news suddenly flashed up on the screen that Merrill Lynch, probably Kevin's biggest client, was being sold to Bank Of America in a rescue package aimed at saving the company. Now, I'm not the sharpest tool in the box, but this was obviously serious. I called Kevin and broke the news to him. He said: "I told you this was going to happen. I should have done something about this last year when I wanted to." In 2007 Premier turned over just under £30m, and Kevin had two verbal offers of £8m and £10m, which he had seriously considered. Now 2008 was looking catastrophic in comparison.

The next day Lehman's Bank had gone. Premier was a minnow in comparison, but considering it took Kevin 20 years to build, it was surprising how quickly it went too. Blue chip companies were dropping like flies, many of whom were customers of Premier and it seemed the staff weren't that keen on hanging around either.

Like any company going through uncertain times, internal politics played a huge role. Some employees were beginning to talk behind others' backs, while others formed different alliances. There was a lot of backstabbing going on too. Paranoia played a big part, and many people were starting to look out for themselves first and foremost.

Kevin was working on a rescue plan to merge Premier Dispatch (the courier firm) and Premier First (the cars and VIP service) - as he described it, "drop one into the other". On paper, there would be a shift of power for some time, which would mean, for a period, all the shares would be owned by Kevin, but this didn't sit well with certain people. Kevin was incensed that he was having to defend himself all the time. Emails criticising his plan were going back and forth. I've never seen him so angry.

In November 2008, we went to Venice for my 35th birthday, to stay at Hotel Danniella, where I'd always wanted to go. When we landed back home a couple of days later, Addison Lee had been in touch, in a bid to buy Premier, hoping to get themselves a bargain deal, given the current and impending economic climate. 'Addi Lee' and Premier were arch rivals and Kevin was now in talks with its boss Liam Griffin. All Kevin wanted was to ensure that the staff all kept their jobs, key people were looked after, and there was something left at the end of it.

In early December 2008 Luc called me on his way to hospital to have eye surgery. "Hi Gucci, it's Luc. I've been trying to get hold of Kevin. Please tell him all the cheque cashing has been done. I'm going in for the op now, but everything is in order." I wished Luc good luck at the hospital, and thought that was that.

Nobody could get hold of Kevin that day because he was down in Devon, looking for a house for us to rent. He knew there would be impending drama over the next few months, and was looking for somewhere for us to hide out, claiming: "We are sitting ducks in this big fucking house". Moment later I got a call from the Premier office, telling me that Luc had resigned by fax.

Luc severing ties with us like that was a massive turning point in our lives, and it's been hard to trust people ever since. It was a big lesson for us to learn, that, sometimes, relationships and friendship aren't enough. Luc had been through so much with me and present throughout so many of my lowest times. He had even taken me to my treatment in Arizona. He had known everything about the possible Addison Lee deal, which was looking more and more likely, because the week before he'd sat in the boardroom while the pros and cons of the deal were discussed. I would like to think he also knew Kevin would look after him whatever happened.

Luc went from being at the birth of our child and Kevin talking to him every day to resigning by fax. He was so close to us that, in a will we were putting together as part of a life insurance policy, we had both provisionally agreed we would like him to have custody of the kids if anything happened to us.

As the credit crunch took its toll Premier now had a big cashflow issue and a huge book debt. Addison Lee offered our bank, who weren't doing great themselves, a deal which meant we kept the house, and a lump sum on top. With Premier, Kevin and I had both signed personal guarantees on the house. We never thought they would be applicable because of the increase in turnover the company was achieving year on year. Kevin did have a plan in place for Premier, but by now, so sick of being bled dry, he simply want to execute it.

In the end, Kevin was happy to accept the Addison Lee deal. He says that Liam Griffin was totally honourable in all dealings he had with him, but while Kevin may have been glad to see the back of his all-consuming company and business life, he was devastated at what he saw as Luc's betrayal.

It was heartbreaking for Kevin, because he was not only losing his firm, but also his best buddy. Kevin doesn't get close to that many people, but he loved that man, only second to me, really. If he was an unapproachable boss, then I could understand it a bit more, but he was a good and generous governor. Kevin's main concern was everyone getting paid on time, and they always did. His word was his bond, and he can't stand it when people don't have the same standards. Even with the Addison Lee deal, he ensured everyone kept their jobs...those who hadn't bailed by then, of course.

The money we did come away with from Premier clearly wasn't going to last forever. The company had now gone, and Gads Hill House wouldn't be far behind it. We got maxed out for a whole host of reasons, and sitting here today, I can honestly say I'm glad we did when we did. We got ripped off in so many ways, and, of course, we made some bad decisions...who doesn't?...but when we had to sell Gads on the cheap, and as a result Kevin sold Premier to Addison Lee for a song, that was the beginning of the end of our ostentatious lifestyle.

I remember us sitting up one night in our huge bedroom at Gads. I was sat on the balcony having a fag and said: "Is this really happening to us Kev?" It broke Kevin's heart because he knew how much I loved that house, but he was adamant we had to sell Gads while we could still get a decent price for it. Nobody knew how long the crunch was going to last, but it clearly wasn't going to end any day soon. The running costs of Gads were huge. We'd done OK out of the Addison Lee deal, but without a business to generate any further income it was prudent to get out while we could. I can now see that Kevin was trying to wean us off that lifestyle, because he knew times were going to get harder and that we needed to move on.

My fairytale had ended and at the time I resented Kevin hugely for that. Now I just wish I hadn't moaned so much. You just don't realise the extreme running costs that go into the upkeep of a house like that. When Kevin had talked about cuts before, he slashed my weekly allowance. He started to rant about tightening our belts so I took it on board in my own inimitable style. On the way through to the West End one morning I dropped him off a packed lunch at the Premier offices. The look on his face was priceless. "Well, that'll make a big fucking difference," he said incredulously.

I'll make no bones about it. I loved those days so much, all the extravagance. When it all came crashing down I thought my life was over. With Premier gone Kevin was convinced we needed to get out of Gads, for our own safety. He reckoned we were exposed as so many people knew where we lived. He'd been down in Devon on a reccy checking out some properties, and schools for the kids - yet another 'geographical' - so we moved out of my dream house on December 30, 2008. The date will be forever engrained on my mind.

It had got to the point just before Christmas, with all the kids presents wrapped under the tree, when we weren't sure whether it was worth them opening them and then having to box them all up again, but we did stay there for Christmas, and then we left. We were a long way from selling Gads yet, but Kevin felt it was better for me to go quickly and get used to the idea that we were selling it. He was keen to liquify our assets while they were still worth something.

We didn't sell the house for another year, but Kevin wanted to keep me away so that when it was sold it was sold. He said it would be easier to move on, and by then we had moved on. Initially there were all sorts of unsavoury people turning up at the house. Kevin joked that we could all be taken down two flights of stairs and locked in the cellar and nobody would have known we were down there for days.

Many so-called friends deserted us. We suddenly realised that we were the people with the gold card, and nobody liked us that much. We always had a house full most Sundays, with everything on tap. Kevin and I were happy to entertain. The way we saw it, there was no point having this big house with just the four of us rattling around. However, when the shit hit the fan, we felt isolated and alone. I know there had been a whispering campaign for a while. It was widely assumed I'd be off if ever the company was in trouble. It was a common perception that I'd bolt at the first sign of Kevin's wealth being at risk...if the money ran out.

None of these people I refer to are in the entertainment industry. In fact, my friends within the business know all about the ups and downs, the peaks and troughs, being in and out of work. The people who stopped ringing are the families we met through the school and some of those who worked for us. I'm a big believer that karma comes around eventually...and what doesn't kill you only makes you stronger.

Not only had the company fallen apart, it caused the family to grow apart too. Kevin had grown close over the years to Eddie, who had now essentially lost his job as well. He and Mum did stay on at the house to keep an eye on things for us. It was hard for them to watch what was happening. They'd seen lots of comings and goings, and had their own thoughts on who had stitched us up over the years There were various candidates, all barring a couple of people - Mark, who was Kevin's right hand man - and Billy Kelly, Kevin's Operations Director. Both were good as gold.

Just before we left Gads the cars started getting picked up, because they had all been leased through Premier. The place became so sad and empty. It felt like I'd fallen from grace again, plunged from my ivory tower. I'd got so used to living in my bubble. I started listening to Radio 4 in the mornings because I thought I should. Then most evenings I'd lay in bed and cry all night because I still couldn't get past certain issues from my previous life as a cocaine addict. I now know the depressive side of bipolar disorder was rampant.

I had to take the kids out of their school, in Kent. I went to see the headmaster, and explained our situation and he said: "I'm seeing so much of this at the moment. Don't worry about your lieu of notice, and I'll make sure you get your deposits back." He was so sweet about it. But the kids seemed so happy there, and I was so happy for them. Kai, in reality, couldn't wait to leave private school...all that wasn't for him. He always had a mohawk haircut or something rebellious that he wasn't allowed. It was clearly time for a massive reality check...just not quite yet.

So next stop Devon, and we still hadn't completely got it We rented a house for the four of us, which again had a pool. We did downgrade our wheels. We got the kids into a lovely village school down there, but we were back up to Gads at the weekends, to see mum and Eddie.

If I'm honest, I tried to be there as much as I could, but I'd be weepy while I cleaned the kitchen, or I'd just go and sit in the garden and blub. Maybe, I told myself, this was my karma, for all the terrible things I'd done and said in my life. Of course, it was all relative because we still had a lovely life in Devon, and I wasn't having to work for it. Kevin was as contented as he could be down there, if not quietly stewing because he didn't have a business to run. He still had a lot of pent-up anger too. He used to say that one of the reasons we were down in Devon was because it was a four hour drive back to London, and if he ever got any silly ideas about rushing back there to deal with anyone who had screwed us along the way, that he would have calmed down by the time he reached them.

I was having to calm down about leaving my dream house. It still upsets me when I think about it, and letting go of it was so hard. I tell you one thing, though. If I ever win the lottery, I'd try to buy that frickin' house again.

DANNIELLA WESTBROOK

11
FAITH

Before we left for Devon I signed up with a new agent called Neil Howarth, from Urban Associates, who I'd been speaking to while Kevin was negotiating the Addi Lee deal. He got me a couple of paid photoshoots, and now he was asking if I'd present a category at the TRIC Awards, held each year by The Television & Radio Industries Club. I accepted and, as luck would have it, there was an *EastEnders* table that night. I chatted briefly to Diederick Santer, the show's new producer, and got on really well with him. Two weeks later Neil got a call. Diederick said: "I want her to come back, and be the original Sam Mitchell."

We were on our way back to London and the kids didn't need asking twice. We had limited money from the sale of Premier, and the house would sell eventually, but Kai and Jodie hated it in Devon. It was winter and they never saw the best of the south west coast. We packed up and headed back, renting a place in Felsted in Essex.

In the April of 2009, my fourth *EastEnders* stint was announced. It would be filmed in two stages over the space of 12 months. I would be replacing my replacement, Kim Medcalf, probably the first time that has ever been done. Kai, meanwhile, attended a state school for the first time, and was at an age when he now understood the jibes the other kids made about mummy's past. The poor thing quickly had to get used to bullying because of my notoriety, especially now I was heading back to Albert Square as well. Kids often taunt him about my nose and addictions. It's hard for him to take at times. Sticks and stones, really. Lots of name calling, but very emotional for any child in that situation. Kai does seem to have a fairly thick skin, but he's only human.

As news of my impending return to *EastEnders* circulated, hey presto, my phone started to ring again...a whole host of so-called friends who had latched on to our luxury lifestyle before, but were nowhere to be seen when it really mattered. You know, they start thinking about the parties they can go to and the premieres they can attend. And I admit I took some of their calls.

Ahead of my *EastEnders'* comeback, Kevin decided to give me the chance to clear the decks. There was also talk of me potentially appearing on the ITV show *Dancing On Ice*. Kevin explained that if I was going to make a double high-profile comeback, in career terms, then this would be a good time to tell him of anything in the past that may come out in the papers, any old flames he didn't know about who may feel tempted to cash in on me being back in the spotlight...any stuff that could embarrass either of us.

We were sitting up in bed one night, and Kevin put it on me. He probably wished he hadn't. It was crunch time. With weeks of filming already completed, my return to Albert Square was about to hit the TV screens and I had now agreed to do *Dancing On Ice*. Kevin wanted me to clear any last remaining skeletons from my closet, and this time I was ready. I knew, alternatively, if it came out in the papers it would break him. In a moment of 'honesty Tourettes' I admitted that I'd been unfaithful. Back in the Spring of 2006, I'd got off with this guy at the wrap party for *Ghost Towns*. I didn't sleep with him, but I crossed the line, all the same.

It was so hard telling Kevin, but I took a deep breath and hoped for the best. The wrap party took place as Kevin and I tried to patch up our relationship after the Bilton episode. I can now see symptoms of bipolar were dominant, and that shouldn't necessarily be an excuse, but, at the time, I was a hot mess and felt completely worthless. Kevin still wasn't convinced I hadn't cheated on him with Bilton. It was as if I copped off with this bloke at the wrap party because, if Kevin didn't believe I hadn't been cheating, then I may as well cheat anyway. All very childish, but in the eye of the storm, and through the pressures of a tough on-the-road job, my defences were down.

We were a small crew at *Ghost Towns*, a friendly team who had bonded over 19 episodes, which had taken us all over the country. I went to the wrap party and got drunk. Plain and simple. Under the backdrop of the Bilton situation, and the doubt already in Kevin's mind, I snogged this guy, and one thing led to another. I was horrified the next morning, and petrified that it would come out in the press any day.

While Kevin admired my honesty...for once...and conceded it was brave to tell him, he was again beside himself. Bittersweet. He says that, looking back, he can now see that something wasn't right around the time I filmed *Ghost Towns*, that despite this wonderful new house I had dreamed of, I still wasn't happy. Certain things just didn't add up. He still says the Bilton situation was harder for him to take, because it was a longer, more premeditated issue, but finding out that I had been unfaithful at a wrap party was devastating for him. He kept saying that this was the first time I was being honest, but at the same time he didn't want to hear any more.

That night there was something else I desperately wanted to tell Kevin. Something far more serious. I had carried the wrap party episode for three years, but I had carried this for almost a decade longer than that. I started to explain how way back in 1994 three dealers who I owed money for drugs had come to my flat and taken me to a house for two days. Kevin was still digesting what had happened at the *Ghost Towns* party, and as I continued, I knew he just wasn't ready for what I was about to tell him. I also thought he may think I was using this latest revelation as a way to get off what I had just told him.

Caught in the moment, encouraged by Kevin saying I was being honest, I thought this was the perfect opportunity to get everything out. However, I knew instinctively I should leave it there. I still wasn't ready either. I certainly didn't have it in me that night to sit up until 5am going through it all, as I knew would surely happen, so I retreated. I said nothing much else happened at the flat, that I did loads of coke with the guys, and they eventually took me home. I told myself it was better I owned *Ghost Towns* first, and came back to the other thing, maybe another day...or maybe never. As we lay there I wasn't sure if Kevin would hang around much longer anyway, but I was convinced telling him any more would definitely send him to the point of no return.

We were both in regular contact with Beechy at this point, and Kevin decided he needed to get away yet again to try and think through this latest bombshell, but this time he didn't check into one of his usual hotels in central London. Beechy suggested he went and stayed with him at his house in France for a couple of weeks, to talk things through, and he did just that.

Kevin says Beechy really helped him at that time, and encouraged him to give me a break, insisting that there may still be deep-rooted issues behind my erratic behaviour, and to remember that the road to recovery was a long and hard one. And Beechy was more than qualified to say that, because, up until that then, he was the only person I had told about being abducted by those dealers, although another abridged version at that.

When Kevin returned from France, he was still in a bad place. I had a week's break in filming at *EastEnders*, so we decided to grab a few days in LA, just the two of us, a perfect opportunity to try and work things out. We had been thinking about relocating to the States for sometime, and if *EastEnders* or *Dancing On Ice* hadn't come up, we may have already been there.

However, the trip didn't start well. As we settled into the first class cabin, and prepared for our plane to take off at Heathrow, Kevin spotted a review of my return to *EastEnders* in one of the Sunday tabloids as we prepared for take off. It likened me to "the Bride Of Chucky". Kevin tried to hide it from me, but I spotted the piece, and it hit me hard. If I had been spotted in Tesco with false eyelashes and a Dynasty hairdo, then fair enough, but Sam Mitchell's tanned and brassy look was vital to the storyline. In any case, did anyone expect me to reappear in Albert Square looking like I did in my 20s? I'd like to say I brushed off the 'Bride Of Chucky' comment, but I didn't and spent most of the flight in tears.

Part of the reason we had gone to LA was to tentatively look at some property out there, now convinced starting afresh in California would be best all round for the family. While we were out and about in the Huntington Beach area we were handed a flyer for a local evangelical church called The Sanctuary. It just so happened to be the same church that our real estate agent Duffy went to. She was an amazing woman, who has been clean 20 years herself, and we fell in love with her immediately. We were viewing some properties on the Saturday, the day before we were leaving and she said we'd love the church and should go along the next morning and give it a try. We were flying home at 9pm on the Sunday, but decided to go because there wasn't much time to do anything else. I'd like to say there was a spiritual calling, but there wasn't. I'd forgotten all about my 'moment' at Cottonwood, where I'd felt something happening to me, so that wasn't in the forefront of my mind. We went because we thought it would be a giggle and we had some time to kill.

I'll admit, Kevin and I were both hoping for some Blues Brothers-type action at The Sanctuary, but we weren't expecting what we did find there. It was mental...set in a big theatre, with Hells Angels, ex-gang members and ordinary families (whatever ordinary is out in LA...) all mixing together. The music was banging and people were dancing in the isles. The atmosphere felt more like a club than a church. It transpired that Duffy had been thrown out of the choir for wearing inappropriate clothing, namely a pair of hot pants, but apart from that it pretty much seemed a case of 'anything goes'. Kevin reckons it was like going to the Ministry Of Sound for the first time and seeing everyone off their heads...or taking your first Ecstasy tablet. And I did get this natural high, the sort of buzz I hadn't felt for a long long time, since I first started taking drugs many years ago. The whole thing just hit us like a brick wall, but it all seemed so genuine too.

When the pastor Jay Haizlip stood up, suddenly everyone sat down and listened intently. He spoke about scripture in modern terms, and we understood it, which was a first. With his tattoos and James Dean style hair, Jay is an enigmatic character. He was saved on the way to a drug deal, and was somebody we could relate to. I'd never wanted anything to do with religion before, not even after Cottonwood, but on the flight home I couldn't stop talking about what we had experienced. Kevin was definitely looking for something, more than I was, so he was naturally hooked, and I think we were now as excited at the prospect of going back to that church, as we were about moving out to LA.

12
THE SQUARE ROUTE

We returned from LA with a spring in our step, the impact of The Sanctuary still overpowering. Our bubble was soon burst when Kevin received word that someone had been given details of our new address, and had been 'booked' to come round and cause him some serious harm. However, it's not often the actual person who has been 'assigned' to do the dirty work lets you know himself. Poor old Kev, if it wasn't me sending the boys round, he was being told of another potential attack, by his own would-be attacker.

The person at the end of the phone was well known to Kevin, someone with a reputation, but there he was, explaining that he had turned down the 'job' because, as he understood, the person who had 'booked' him had been well looked after by Kevin in the past. And, without naming names, he was right. This guy told Kevin that he had been offered a hefty payment and a free holiday for his services, but that he couldn't and wouldn't do it, purely out of principle. He was quoting the address of our new house, the address of the place in Devon, which very few people had known, and every other we'd lived in since we'd met. Kevin knows who was behind this, and once again, the new Kevin had to keep his calm. It was like something out of a soap opera, like something out of *EastEnders*...which was exactly where I was heading next.

I thought I'd left Albert Square for good. Returning gave me the perfect opportunity to see and work with everybody again free from drugs, and also to apologise to anyone I'd compromised during my previous stints on the show, which was practically everyone. I was picked ahead of Kim Medcalf because of my supposed on-screen presence with Sid Owen and Patsy Palmer, who as Ricky and Bianca would both be central to the new storyline, and I felt fortunate to be given yet another stab at the role. Sam Mitchell was and is such part of my life. It was great to have her back.

Returning to Albert Square is always a huge experience. I wouldn't say I was nervous, because I feel so at home at the studios in Borehamwood. However, with my bipolar issues unresolved, I did have the odd moment of anxiety. There are plenty of familiar faces all over the set, from the everyday staff to the production crew and, of course, the cast. One actor I hadn't appeared in the soap with yet was Jake Wood, who plays Max Branning. Following drugs and addiction issues with me and other young actors, bosses at *EastEnders* had now set up a mentor system. Sam had little to do with Max, storyline-wise, so I was assigned to Jake. We got on fabulously. He was always on hand, having a coffee with me in the square when we weren't filming, and meeting me for lunch once a week in the canteen to make sure I was OK. I can't thank Jake enough, and he's been a constant source of support to me ever since.

My return, like my life in general, received mixed reviews. Stuart Heritage of *The Guardian* wrote on the recasting of Sam in June 2010: *"Medcalf lacked Westbrook's obvious aura of constant threat, but still managed to help bludgeon Dirty Den's head before leaving."* Kevin O'Sullivan for the *Sunday Mirror* was critical, highlighting an *"inexplicable personality transplant"* in Sam. He labelled my return as: *"an insult to long-suffering viewers' intelligence".* Another review on the Virgin Media website rated my return as the tenth greatest soap comeback of all time, adding: *"She was only on screen for five seconds before the famous 'Enders drums signalled the return of Walford's much-missed Mitchell sister."*

Coming back to *EastEnders* also presented me with another embarrassing situation...a bed scene with Scott Maslen. Now, I appreciate that there's a lot of women out there who wouldn't see that as an issue at all, so bear with me. The dreaded screen kiss or TV bed scene is the bane of any actor's life. What can appear as a sensual moment is a cold and calculated process, filmed over several takes in front of a room full of cameramen and production crew. Where *EastEnders* is concerned, it's very cold. It can be freezing on that set, so a pair of thick socks is always in order.

Scott Maslen is very popular with the ladies, and was voted 'Sexiest Male' in the Soap Awards for four consecutive years, between 2009 and 2012. When Scott was in The Bill I loved a bit of DS Phil Hunter, as Kevin well knew, and could be heard mumbling "phwoarrr...what a sort!!!" if he appeared on the screen. Sam Mitchell was coming back this time to try and resurrect her relationship with Ricky. Her exit in 2005 was the conclusion of a big storyline which saw her wrongly imprisoned for the murder of Den Watts. After eventually being cleared, and fleeing the country, Sam was now back on Albert Square, battling Bianca for Ricky, and also about to embark on an affair with Jack Branning, played by a certain Scott Maslen. I wasn't aware of this fact when I first came back, but as the plot unravelled Sam eventually got her wicked way with Jack.

In the whole time I acted with Sid Owen, Sam and Ricky probably had about three full-on screen snogs. The scriptwriters eventually gave up on us, because when it came to a kiss on the lips, Sid and I would either start laughing or bickering. I just couldn't go there. After many years, it simply didn't feel right snogging Sid. I remember when I first joined the soap. I was sitting in the canteen with Michelle Gayle, who I knew from my days in *Grange Hill*. Sid shouted over with a mouthful of bacon sandwich: "Oi, 'Chelle, has she got the Sam Mitchell role?" Michelle nodded and Sid looked me up and down and said: "Yeah, she'll do." He knew I was going to be his love interest, and it was funny that he was blatantly sizing me up and talking about me, not to me. We got on so well and so quickly, that a brotherly sisterly relationship developed. We always found any intimate scenes tricky because we had literally grown up together.

Sam hooking up with Jack Branning would be a completely different prospect altogether. She had already had a stormy relationship with Beppe di Marco, and Michael Greco, who played the role, was a good mate of Kevin's when we met, so getting intimate with 'Grecs' back then was always weird too. Now, I was about to film a bed scene with Scott, and Kevin wound me up something rotten about my old crush.

Fortunately, it wasn't the first time I'd met Scott. When he was still in The Bill we bumped into him at the premiere to Danny Dyer's *Football Factory* film, and he introduced us to his wife Estelle, who is lovely.

Kevin does admit that, when I'm acting, he finds that part of the business difficult, as any husband or partner not involved in the business would. Neither of us watch anything that I'm in when it's screened. I certainly wouldn't watch any scenes of myself when I'm kissing anyone....it would be like watching your mum and dad kissing...unbearable! To compound things, I hadn't long come clean about the *Ghost Towns* wrap party, so anything that involved kissing another man was always going to be delicate.

Sometimes, with this sort of thing, it's the whole process that can be difficult to deal with. I found myself one Thursday night, laying in bed with Kevin, reading my script for the next day's filming with *EastEnders*, realising that the bed scene was the next morning, and fibbing about it. "The bed scene's in a couple of weeks," I assured Kevin. In my mind, I thought I was avoiding a difficult weekend. A classic case, as Kevin says, of me "lying when the truth will do". In reality, Kevin deals well with these sorts of things, so I was just over-thinking it all. When I got home the next night, with the bed scene in the can, I joked with Kevin about it and we quickly moved on.

That liaison with Scott typified TV bed scenes in general. We were laying there with cups of tea, our phones and our scripts. On cue, you give your tea to someone, put your phone under the covers and tuck the script under a pillow. Under those sheets, on that occasion, Scott just had his Calvin Kleins on, because he needed to get out of the bed in the scene, but I was wearing a bikini top, tracksuit bottoms and my trusty woolly socks. It's about as unglamorous as you can get.

Scott is a great guy, and a real family man. Conversely, his character Jack has had all the Mitchell girls...Sam and her cousins Roxi and Roni. I remember speaking to Rita Simons, who plays Roxi, about my first kiss scene with Scott. Rita is a great friend of mine, and we were like 'besties' comparing notes. She assured me that once Scott started talking about fishing I would lose all my inhibitions, and just get on with the job in hand.

However, no disrespect to Scott, but I'd long reeled in my biggest catch in the TV kissing stakes...one Martin Kemp, way back in the '90s, when Sam had a fling with his character Steve Owen. I was in my mid-20s and that kiss was THE real knee trembler. I'd never kissed a real man before, and such an iconic pop star at that. I was still only used to dating boy band singers, wearing baggy jeans and beanie hats. Working with Martin is not like preparing for a screen kiss with Sid Owen or Scott Maslen. Both those guys are great fun, and always joking around before the take, and that helps relax the situation. Martin, however, is a true professional. He comes on set, has already learned his lines, and is quickly in character. He's such a lovely man, but he's not there to muck around, he's there to get the job done. He's very studious and calculated, just how he came across in *Celebrity Big Brother*, but he's also a total heartthrob where I'm concerned. I'm old enough to remember growing up with *Spandau Ballet* in their prime, and I'm also a massive fan of the film *The Krays* Martin and his brother Gary starred in.

For the Sam and Steve snog *EastEnders* bosses were getting their money's worth again out of me. They've had me dressed up in all sorts of things over the years, and often dolled up to the nines. I was once dumped out onto Albert Square in my undies by Bianca. This time they had me dressed up as Miss Christmas, in a sexy red and white corset and stockings and suspenders. I had to walk up and down the bar like that, and seduced Steve Owen in the process. I remember Tamzin Outhwaite, who was playing Steve's then on-screen love interest Melanie being so supportive. This scene was the last of the day and I was nervous so Tamzin said she'd wait for me, and watch me on one of the monitors. I came straight out to her afterwards, blushing and smiling at the same time, whispering: "Oh, my God." "I know," Tamzin said. "It's great isn't it?" I got straight on the phone to my mum, and told her: "I've just snogged Martin Kemp." "You lucky cow," came back the response.

I'm always asked if I would consider going back to *EastEnders*, and the answer is always an emphatic: "Yes". The result of my affair with Jack saw me give birth to his child, and means Sam is a Mitchell with a Branning baby. With those two families constantly at war and intertwined in most modern day plots I guess there's a chance they may want to bring Sam back.

13
THIN ICE

The first part of my last *EastEnders* comeback wasn't screened until September 2009, by which time I was on the verge of leaving again, in filming terms, and heading for my new incarnation...that of a contestant on *Dancing On Ice*. I'd always watched the show. In fact, I was hooked from the first series. When I was asked to take part, I didn't have to think twice. As well as being taught a skill, there's the compulsory spray tans and loads of sparkles. What girl wouldn't be up for that? But, boy, do you have to work hard! It's relentless at times. Pretty much 6am - 10pm, seven days a week...for months.

Compared to *I'm A Celebrity...Get Me Out Of Here*, there are no comparisons. *'I'm A Celeb'* turns your brains to mush. If you're like me...and you feel a bit tortured...the jungle is a dangerous place to be. It's so dull in there it highlights everybody's flaws. The main reason I did the show was because of Ant & Dec. They're such brilliant hosts...amazing at what they do. But *I'm A Celeb* and *Big Brother*, to a certain extent, are both designed to destroy you. *Dancing On Ice* and *Strictly Come Dancing*, on the other hand, are both creative processes which teach the contestants a skill.

With *Dancing On Ice* you just don't have time to get bored. With I'm A Celeb and *Big Brother*, you literally have hours on your hands, and it does your head in. I was invited to interview for a place on the January 2013 *Celebrity Big Brother* series and, at that time I just wasn't feeling it. I had such a difficult time in the jungle, that I know I came across really badly when I met the CBB producers, and could feel myself trying to put them off me.

Like I'm A Celeb, the viewers love it if someone has a breakdown in the BB house, and it wasn't going to be me that time. I watched Denise Welsh lose the plot the year before, and I was determined not to put myself in that position. My sanity was worth so much more. I did appear as a panelist on the spin-off show, *Big Brother's Bit On The Side*, for that series, and a lot of people there were calling for me to be in the next CBB, but I'm not sure that sort of show is for me any more. It was great to see Rylan shine through in that CBB series. I first met him on ITV's *Daybreak* show when he was involved in a Katie Price TV show, a year before he was on *X-Factor*. He's a great guy, and I got on with him well. Rylan works so hard at whatever he's doing and deserves all the success that comes his way.

With *Dancing On Ice*, just like *Strictly Come Dancing*, there are always a couple of stars with experience or the general aptitude to do well, then two or three people who have at least skated or danced at a very basic level when they were young. Those four or five contestants usually make up the semi-finalists, with the most proficient person usually taking the crown. I had skated a bit as a kid with my mates, but I was rubbish at dancing at stage school. I was always in the bottom group and told to stand at the back for musical theatre. But I made the commitment that I would give the show 100 per cent, enjoy it and make the most of it. Hopefully that came across in my performances.

For me, the best thing about *Dancing On Ice* was working with Torville and Dean...Chris and Jane, those two iconic Olympians. I'm from that generation who grew up watching their gold medal routines, when they were national heroes, when the whole of the UK stopped to see what they had come up with next. I remember when they did 'Bolero', it was a massive national TV event. I could never have imagined that I would get the chance to skate with them, let alone be taught by them and have them come up with new routines for me each week.

Before that my first session with *Dancing on Ice* was at the Lee Valley Ice Rink, where the show would film the announcement of who my skate partner was. Matthew Gonzalez skated out, with amazing dazzling white teeth, looking like a Disney Prince. And it turned out he was once a prince, at Disneyland. Matt and I got on so well from day one, and the fact that we knew the area in

California where he'd grown up so well from our trips out there meant we clicked immediately.

Matt was a new skater to the show, so I think that helped because it was the first day for both of us. We started in October, a month later than most of the contestants, because of my *EastEnders* commitments. I had managed to do some initial training at the rink at Riverside Leisure Centre in Chelmsford, close to where we were living. The main man there John Wicker had dragged me round the ice a few times. Then I had several sessions with Karen Barber, one of the show's judges, and Mark Naylor, who is Robin Cousin's partner. When we teamed up with Chris and Jane I was so in awe...and it didn't help that they had to catch me when I first skated up to them. They're so lovely, though, and as gracious and generous as they appear on TV.

Matt and I quickly settled into a routine...but not before I sorted out his living arrangements. He had been put him up in a pokey flat at Elstree Studios. When I saw it I was horrified. It was too basic, with a crappy little TV in the corner and no Wi-Fi. Matt had come from this lovely area in California, and was now in this dingy little place next to the Big Brother house. I told him to pack his bags...he was coming to stay with us. By then we were at a lovely house out in Great Leighs and had an annexe that he could stay in so it just made sense.

Matt was a super hard worker, and got on great with Kevin and the kids. Our routine was relentless. We started at 6.30 each morning in Chelmsford, then moved on to Elstree for our allotted two hour session on the ice at the studios. Then it was back to Chelmsford for more skating until 9pm at night. We weren't back home until at least 10pm, then it was back up there again first thing. John Wicker was over the moon, because us practicing at the rink in Chelmsford was such great profile for him. And it was fitting because he had taught me at the start. I got him and his wife tickets for all the live shows. They never missed one. I still go up to Chelmsford and skate there and see them both.

Right at the start, Matt asked me how hard I was prepared to work. I said: "I'll work as hard as I possibly can. I really want to nail this." But the skating was difficult, and learning all the routines was punishing. There never seemed to be enough time in the week. We would get our routines on a Monday. Chris and Jane would work them out from scratch, in front of us...which was fascinating. They know each other so well and are ultimate professionals. On hand the whole time was Maxine, Chris and Jane's physio since the Olympics. I broke three ribs in week three and also popped my knee during a country and western routine, but there was no chance I was pulling out. I loved doing that show too much. It is easily the best job I've ever had.

Matt was such a good friend to me, and still is. We had such a laugh, he made it so fun. Skating live on TV is just so much more nerve-wracking than pre-recording a soap opera. Matt said the best way to get round the fear of skating was to act my way through it. And acting did help massively. The producer, Paul, told me that I always hit my red lights and picked out the next camera...whatever position I was in...bang, bang, bang. Matt also said we should leave any arguments on the ice. He didn't just teach me to skate, he held me up mentally. When I left I took Matt on GMTV with me. Not many people take their partners, but we were a team, that's the way I saw it. We were the first couple to skate on the first live show for our series. I spent the hour before telling my runner Dominic: "Get me a cab, I can't do it...I'm not doing it..." In fact, Chris and Jane were genuinely worried we weren't going to do it.

The highlight for me was the Dusty Springfield routine. Also the props week with the chair, where we danced to *You've Got The Look*. We got to the top that week, the only week anyone beat the eventual winner, *Emmerdale* actress Hayley Tamaddon. That was a real high. The funny thing was Matt was so young he hardly knew any of the old tracks we had to dance to. Our progress was great, and as people started dropping out, we made it to the last four, along with Hayley, Gary Lucy, a good old Loughton boy, and Kieran Richardson, who I went on to act with on Hollyoaks. When we reached the quarter-finals we got to skate with Torville and Dean on the live shows. The boys skated with Jane and Hayley and I got to skate with Chris. It was immense...I was like: "I'm skating with Christopher 'frickin' Dean.

I was just delighted to make the last four, and the overall experience was amazing. I made so many friends and have kept in touch with everyone. I enjoyed the *Dancing On Ice* experience so much more than the jungle. All the other contestants were lovely. Danny Young and Kieran were like my kids. Sharon Davies was also on my show...she was brilliant, and also Tana Ramsay. I got on really well with her. Everyone was so nice from the crew to the presenters. Karen Barber and I bonded over our love of Jo Malone candles. Each week Philip Schofield would be shouting through my dressing room wall: "I know you're in there Westbrook. I can smell those candles from here."

The other person I loved working with was Heather Mills. I try not to prejudge people because that's always happened to me. She was just so nice, a warm person who adores her child. She was always bringing in treats for us, like homemade biscuits, and texting ahead to see if anybody wanted a coffee brought in. Everybody makes her out to be a gold digger, but she seems anything but. I had so much admiration for her, skating with that prosthetic leg. She's now training to ski with the Great Britain Paralympics team, and hopes to compete at the Winter Olympics in Russia in 2014. She won four gold medals at a top championships in the States so things are looking good for her. If she makes the games it will be a massive achievement. I love the way Heather takes all the flak she gets with a pinch of salt, and find that so inspiring.

Each show there was me, Heather and Sharon, the older ones, the mums, gassing before the show. We were all friends, there was no rivalry between us. However, when it came to announcing who was leaving you could cut the tension with a knife. Each week we were all desperate to stay. Some of the younger ones would be on their mobiles as soon as they finished, voting for themselves again and again.

But there was a price for all this. I had hardly seen Kevin for months, and we still had lots to talk about, and go through. As the show neared its conclusion, the pressure on my family started to takes its toll. I was simply never around. I was working on routines all week, and on the show all weekend...Saturday and Sunday. For five months everything had been about *Dancing On Ice*. Everything else had seemed irrelevant. Kevin still had the fall-out of the business to deal with and my *Ghost Towns* wrap party revelations left him stunned. I had alluded to that even more harrowing event deep in my past, but there had simply been no time to talk about all the issues that had been raked up recently.

There had been so much pressure on the family, and we just weren't structured to deal with a live show each week. The kids had only recently joined new schools again, they were having to make new friends and were fed up with being pulled from pillar to post. Each Sunday night Kevin and the kids would be wheeled out to support me, and literally had to be all smiles as the camera panned to them when I was about to skate. I don't think the public realise just how much of a strain shows like *Dancing On Ice* and *Strictly Come Dancing* place on the contestants. Sure, we're all eager to sign up, and I did have the time of my life, but it's no surprise that so many relationships don't survive those shows.

Towards the end of my stint on *Dancing On Ice* our therapist Beechy held a summit in the kitchen at our house. Kevin had been seeing Beechy a lot during that time, talking through the *Ghost Towns* situation, and how best to deal with me. There were still major issues over the Premier sale. There was a dispute between two creditors, which Kevin knew would eventually be sorted out amicably, but not if he was stuck in the middle. In fact, he believed it would cost him a couple of hundred thousands pounds if he was in the mix. That added to his continued turmoil about my confessions meant he was desperate to get away.

I nipped out to get some kebabs, and when I got back Beechy was suggesting that Kevin head to LA, to Huntington Beach. We'd been out there a few months earlier looking at property, with a view to moving, and had stumbled across The Sanctuary, this exciting evangelical church there. With me so busy it made sense for Kevin to head to LA, hire a car, and gather his thoughts again away from the eye of the storm. However, whether he even wanted to be with me, let alone start a new life in the States, was questionable once more. Beechy was insistent this was best all round, and so plans were put in place.

Out in LA, Kevin was in daily contact with Beechy. The more Kevin thought about it the more he believed the relationship was over. In the last year or so he had lost his business, his best mate and loads of other long-standing relationships built up during the life of Premier, and then had been hit with my infidelity. It was one thing after another...and another. He told Beechy what his current state of mind was and by the time I got through to Kevin he was telling me he wanted a divorce.

I was still seeing Beechy loads too so with any drama like this I would naturally give him a call. Amazingly, he told me to go ahead, and break up, that he actually thought Kevin was selfish for deserting me during such an important TV show. I couldn't believe what he was saying, but I trusted him so much that I began to think about it seriously.

Beechy insisting that I agree to the split with Kevin just seemed so weird. Then when Kevin was back from LA for my last Dancing On Ice show we finally had a chance to sit down and talk about it face to face, and it all seemed to click into place. It was like Beechy was playing us off against each other. He had suggested Kevin went to LA and then told me he was selfish for leaving. He apparently told Kevin I had a housekeeper so I would be fine, and that I was just too wrapped up in my career to save our marriage.

When the penny dropped we were distraught. Beechy had stopped picking up Kevin's calls by now, saying that he had dropped his phone in his pool. It just all got more bizarre by the day. I showed Kevin the texts I had from Beechy and what he had been saying about him. He was fuming. "He knows you've got bipolar, he knows your history," he said. Beechy had sent Kevin to LA, but all the time was telling me to finish *Dancing On Ice*, and then come out and join him in France, so he could "work through my issues". Kevin had been out there earlier in the year. I saw him on and off for ten years. At £100 an hour...you do the math!

We trusted Beechy so much we did couples therapy together, and he even saw Kai a few times. If he was flying into Stansted at short notice, Beechy would come and stay with us. We classed him as a close family friend. The hurt we felt still cuts deep. Kevin had been seeing him on and off for a year. Unbeknown to me, he says Beechy was telling him I was a nightmare - "once an addict, always an addict" - at the same time saying to me: "Please keep what we talk about confidential, even to Kevin, you know what he's like...very manipulative."

To some extent Beechy was telling me what I wanted to hear. I came back from Dancing On Ice one night, ran a big bubble bath, and I was sitting on the bathroom floor, thinking: "I'm doing a live TV show, trying my best to be a mum, and my marriage is falling apart...my therapist is telling me to leave my husband, and I can't talk to anybody else about it."

When I did report back to Kevin it seemed that everything I said contradicted what he had been told. That made us row even more. Kevin was saying: "Have you been speaking to him? Are you bullshitting me about going to therapy? Have you been missing appointments again?". When my bipolar is at its worst I believe everything I'm told. Kevin was incensed. There had been people on the sidelines trying to make money out of him for years, and now he felt Beechy was trying to turn us over too. Out of all the people we felt let us down, Beechy hurts the most. I think it's true that to many people we were worth more apart, and then there was also money in getting us back together...and, who knows?...apart again.

I was devastated. We both were. I dedicated my first book to Beechy, and he even came up with the name for it. He said: "You've been nowhere, now you're the other side of nowhere." He'd dealt with me in all of my darkest moments. I'd be totally fucked on coke and on the phone saying: "I think I'm about to die. I've taken crack." I'd visit him shaking, with cocaine itches and he would talk me through it. Man, I trusted him so much. I used to lie on his couch, and literally sob for hours.

I'm one of his real success stories, but I believe he sold me out. Beechy saved my life to a certain degree. When the stories came out in the *News Of The World* about him making advances on his female patients I stood up for him. I have to say he was 100% professional with me, and I never saw that side to him, but he did eventually get struck off.

Kevin and I used to stay with him and his wife, and go to horse shows together. It was heartbreaking. I had a miscarriage 18 months after Jodie was born, and I went straight to him about it. I was pregnant, with no nose, getting flown out to the States for last-chance saloon treatment, on the front of the papers, and Beechy got good press out of that. Sure he stood my ground for me, but sometimes you wonder how much you're worth to people once you're finally in recovery.

Kevin's therapist Erol, who he met at The Priory.... he was amazing. I even started seeing him, and he used to get so much more out of me than Beechy. He'd look me in the eye and I'd think: "Please don't ask me a question, because you'll know I'm not telling the truth." In hindsight I would have got a lot more done with Erol in a shorter space of time, but he was suddenly diagnosed with cancer and gone within six weeks. We were heartbroken, and that's when Kevin started seeing Beechy.

Thankfully, when all the pieces fell into place, Kevin and I started to put our differences to one side again. Kevin sent Beechy a text message, explaining how disappointed we both were, and we've had nothing to do with him since. The worst thing is that I trusted Beechy with my darkest moments, things I hadn't even told my parents...or Kevin fully.

14
A FRESH START

The move to LA was still on, but only just.

The morning after Matt and I were voted off *Dancing On Ice* I was in the kitchen at home, with Kevin demanding a divorce. Two hours later I was sat on the sofa on ITV's *This Morning* with Matt talking to Philip Schofield about time on the show....explaining how I couldn't have made it that far without the support of my family...putting a brave face on it all, letting the inner actress in me take over.

I really had to persuade Kevin to give our relationship and family one last go. The whole *Dancing On Ice* experience had left us fractured at best. Before we could move anywhere, straight after *Dancing On Ice* I had my final stint in *EastEnders* to complete - 17 episodes that were filmed in the Spring of 2010, and aired between August and September of that year. The last was my 270th *EastEnders* episode in total. With filming finished, I continued to work on Kevin, begging him to give this dream new life in LA a go. I honestly believed that quality time out in Huntington Beach as a family away from the pressure of my recent fame, and all my trials and tribulations back in the UK, made so much sense. I did all

I could to remind him about The Sanctuary and how upbeat we had felt after our experience at that church. Fortunately, yet again, he gave in.

When we did finally move we quickly settled in Huntington Beach and became regulars at The Sanctuary, but we didn't get to know the church's figurehead Jay Haizlip immediately. The Senior Pastor there, Jay's such a cool guy. He's had all sorts of addictions himself and and was a pro-skateboard and model. He's definitely not your average pastor. First we got to know a couple called Brian and Tracey Sumner. Brian, a champion skateboarder too, was a greeter and deacon at the church, and is originally from Liverpool, so he was keen to welcome this new English couple. His wife Tracey is from LA, but the fascinating thing about Brian was that he had been in California since he was 16 touring with skate legend Tony Hawk and knew nothing about my fame through *EastEnders* or anything about me.

The other interesting thing about Brian and Tracey was their own relationship. They had met and married in their late teens, and with a young son called Dakota, divorced several years later. It was only after Brian discovered his own faith, and he and Tracey both started attending The Sanctuary, that they got back together and eventually remarried. Brian had teamed with Jay to form The Uprising, a skateboard ministry, which led to an award-winning reality TV show and Brian's own organisation SkateBible. He now speaks about his faith all over the world, so by hooking up with him and Tracey as soon as we moved out to LA we got a first class modern-day Christian education, and one that we could relate to.

Kevin believes strongly that God saved us both when we met at the boxing event all those years before, and that he also sent us to The Sanctuary. Brian and Tracey were so welcoming, and invested so much of their time in us. We had come from a spiritually barren material world, and they helped us grow as a family unit. By now they had two other children, Eden and Jude. We lived a couple of blocks away from each other, and very close to the beach, so we would all hang out there loads. Brian and Kevin would get into these deep and crazy religious conversations and Tracey would have separate chats with me, equally as spiritual in their own way.

And it's simple. The church changed the way we think, the way we live and the way we treat people. Since Kevin changed his lifestyle he's always been curious about religion and faith. If he was a prime candidate for being saved, then I'd like to think I too was looking for something else, and a better way to exist. I'd certainly believe we are less self-obsessed now. Kevin took to it immediately, but then he generally only does one speed. He always dives off the top board. What I found amazing was how the bible quickly became all-consuming for Kevin. Due to his dyslexia he had only ever read two books, and he cannot remember any of the central characters. Suddenly he was reading the bible, and quoting all sorts from it.

Personally, I've always seen the church, first and foremost, as being about community, and that's where my faith comes in, with people. I'm not trying to tell anybody about God. I think my christianity is more about people, and helping. Back in the day, when I staggered out of Browns or wherever in the early hours of the morning with a group of friends, I was always the one giving the homeless guy a tenner, while everyone else sniggered and sneered. I believe I've always had a heart. I think I was just always so self-obsessed that it rarely got a chance to shine through.

After effortlessly settling in at The Sanctuary we eventually got to know Jay and his family well too. His wife Christy came with me to see my old Dancing On Ice partner Matt in the US version of the show, *Skating With The Stars*, and our relationship developed from there. The Sanctuary was an exciting place to be, but also a calming influence on all of us too.

I was just enjoying being a mum, though, and doing stuff with the family, away from the pressures of my notoriety in the UK. And as far as acting went, it's strange, but I just wasn't interested out there. I certainly had the contacts for it. Our mate Michael Greco was in LA, trying to build his profile and have a stab at acting. Grecs is making some progress as well, and starred in three-part TV mini series *Hatfields & McCoys* with Kevin

Costner, not to mention winning big on the *World Series Of Poker*. We'd all go and watch Grecs play football with Vinnie Jones. Jason Statham would come and hang out, and so would Piers Morgan.

By the time I got to LA I was already good friends with Sharon Osbourne, another massive British star who has made her name in the States. I first met Sharon and Ozzy Osbourne a couple of years earlier through my hairdresser Lino Carbosiero, who is one of the head stylists at Daniel Galvin in the West End. Lino's clients include the likes of David Cameron and Sam Cam, Hilary Clinton, Ant & Dec and Patsy Kensit. I was at the salon just behind Selfridges and made my way down from having my colour done upstairs, to the downstairs area where Lino cuts. There were three seats, and Sharon and Ozzy were sitting in two of them. I exchanged pleasantries, sat down and picked up a magazine. When I went to the toilet a few minutes later Ozzy was teetering on the edge of his seat, craning to get a look at me and saying to Sharon: "Is that, err, you know, err...?" in that unmistakable voice of his. Sharon was hilarious, and barked at him: "Yes it is, now shut up." I was creasing up in the toilets and chuffed to bits that Ozzy had recognised me. When I got back to my seat Sharon and I started talking and we clicked immediately. We really hit it off, swapped numbers and have kept in touch ever since.

I was already a massive fan of *The Osbournes*, which launched a whole genre of reality shows and paved the way for the likes of *Keeping Up With The Kardashians*. Sharon was already someone I admired and looked up to hugely, and she's such a lovely lovely person, one of the most genuine people you could meet. When we moved out to LA our friendship naturally developed further. She was judging on *America's Got Talent* at the time and is also a presenter of *The View*, the American version of ITV's *Loose Women*. I loved going up to see Sharon when she was filming these shows. Going to a TV studio on a social basis, not having to work when I got there, was so refreshing in itself. Afterwards we'd hang out in Sharon's trailer, and she told me that she just enjoyed having a gossip with a fellow Brit over a cup of tea. I get that, because LA can seem so different to the UK at times. You often need that connection with someone from back home to help you chill out.

One time Ozzy was doing a book signing at a Barnes & Noble store in Huntington Beach, near our home, so Sharon came down too, and we had a catch-up over some sushi. We were also invited to the premiere of Jack Osbourne's film *God Bless Ozzy Osbourne*, which is a beautiful piece of work.

While Sharon has been a life mentor to me, I would consider Barbara Windsor as my career mentor. I've learned so much from Barbara, and June Brown, about acting. I'm so lucky to have had Barbara in my life. She has been so good at showing me how the industry worked, and been such a friend to me. When I was ill she kept in contact with my mum. Like Sharon, she has never judged me, she simply cared. I have such a huge respect for Barbara and her door has always been open.

Meanwhile, the Americans can't get enough of Sharon Osbourne. You think she's a big star in the UK, but even more so in the States. She epitomises the American Dream, a strong woman who has worked hard for her success. Sharon is so much about her family too, and so caring. Like me, she loves her dogs. She always checks in from time to time...sends me a personal tweet or a text every now and then. When I was in *Dancing On Ice*, Sharon was so supportive. She is such a massive role model for me. She has always encouraged me to tell the truth. She has been so honest about her own life and is one of the reasons I've been so honest in this book.

Out in LA I officially had a new role model in my life. God!

But this was hardly a conventional introduction to Christianity. The evangelical churches in LA are fascinating, filled with colourful characters. I quickly hit it off with Jay's wife Christy, and, bless her, she's not your average pastor's wife...she's rock-chick trendy and great looking, but also a strong woman of God.

For me, the initial attraction of The Sanctuary was all the drama, and enough people that were possibly as infamous and notorious as me, in their own right. Loads of cool people. Katy Perry's parents, Keith and Mary, they are travelling pastors, and regular speakers at The Sanctuary. We got held back one week to meet them.

If a lot of the churches in LA are far from conventional, then neither is my faith. I struggle with it because I can't see it, touch it or watch it...and it doesn't talk to me like Kevin says his does to him. Apart from finding it impossible to believe I can be forgiven for all my sins, I generally don't trust things very easily anyway. But I embraced my new-found faith, and it was new-found. I've always believed in God. I didn't know him, but I often talked to him, and I think people do that, whatever they're going through, even if they're not spiritually aware. In their darkest moments the person they call upon is God. We were fledgling Christians, and make no mistake, this exciting and unpredictable church in LA was where we were saved. Kevin says he witnessed me praying for up to 20 minutes several times, with my arms in the air, and witnessed first hand the spirit entering me, even if I can't quite ever remember it like that.

The first time I joined Twitter was in LA, recommended by Jay, in fact, and in the first few weeks I tweeted him a message saying "Thank you for leading me to the Lord." I still wasn't quite sure how it worked with Twitter, that within a couple of weeks I had several hundred followers back in the UK, and that some of them were journalists. Suddenly there were paps turning up at house, and reporters sitting in the row behind us at church.

In July 2011, an LA-based journalist from one of the national newspapers in the UK, was the first to approach me about an article talking about my faith, and I decided if I was going to do it I would donate my fee to The Sanctuary. We had already started contributing financially anyway, as is common for the members of any congregation of any church the world over. We still seemed fairly comfortably off so it made perfect sense, and I started to negotiate a fee for the article of around $5,000. It was the usual idea. If I could do one piece talking about my faith, then the rest of the newspapers could glean what they wanted and hopefully the other reporters would stop coming to the church and the paps would leave us alone once more.

Eventually I opted to do an exclusive with Dean Piper at *The Daily Mirror*, who I've always had a good relationship with. As this was another delicate subject and time in my life I felt more comfortable going with someone I knew. I fully expected there would be cynicism surrounding any revelations of me discovering God or being saved. I was sure that would come with the territory, it usually does with anything to do with me. Dean did a great job, a lovely article, but the other paper ran a largely disparaging and skeptical piece about my faith the following day. Insinuating that I was unable to leave my old lifestyle behind simply because I made a trip to *America's Got Talent* with Christy to see Sharon Osbourne was also pushing it a bit far. It's not like I was falling out of LA's notorious club The Viper Room, off my head again.

The very fact we were based out in LA meant we were able to move on a lot quicker than if we had been back home. Other papers did leave us alone after that, and we really began to settle into LA life, and the new community we had been welcomed into in and around the church. Kevin had a spiritual experience with one of the deacons there, Greg DeVries, who is now a pastor. Greg told him that God wanted him to know he had seen everything he had been through, and that his wife will get well, but it would take time...that it would be a process. And I had certainly been a process, alright. Fortunately I had convinced Kevin to give me some more time

And if it was time we needed, we couldn't have picked a better setting. Huntington Beach is beautiful. It's not a flashy part of LA. Everybody goes to the gym, or runs or surfs and there's a lot of MMA (Mixed Martial Arts) fighters down there, so Kevin and Kai were in their element. It's very family orientated. Everybody takes their kids (and dogs) everywhere. In the UK, you have to visit one of those crappy restaurants with the balls if you want to eat out with young children. In LA, it's the norm to rock up at a cool sushi place and have lunch with your children or Pitbull or with your toy dog in your bag.

Nobody ever gets that dressed up, it's a relaxed uniform of T-Shirts, vests, shorts...whatever. Although I'm more of a pool person, as a family, we naturally spent a lot of time on the beach. Both the kids learned to surf and body board. It was a total different way of life out there and we all loved it. Jodie even developed a full-on Californian accent. We couldn't be happier.

Initially being in LA was so refreshing because nobody there knew who I was or anything about my past, and the Californians are just not as judgmental as people in the UK. Nobody befriended me because they wanted anything from us, and I think our time there helped mould me into the person that I was meant to be, and helped define our family unit too. Importantly, Kai wasn't someone's kid, he was just Kai. In fact, I felt it was the first time the kids could be themselves. The first time their classmates weren't telling them about their junkie mother. Kids back in the UK had even put up posters of the 'nose' picture around Kai's school. Even Kevin's daughter Jordan has taken shit about me over the years.

In some ways, I think many parts of Essex are more pretentious than LA. Out there they don't care if you're driving a Bentley or riding a skateboard. Essex is so much more obviously plastic now than it used to be. It sounds strange after all the money I've spent on designer gear, but after living in LA I couldn't believe how much the UK relies on its status symbols.

Out in LA, we had been given the right platform spiritually, but the madness in our lives still continued. We still had a lot of things to work through. My as yet untreated bipolar could flare up at any moment. Not ideal, as we were in the process of setting up a dog-grooming business there.

Opening Barkingham Palace was a dream come true for me. It was something completely different to acting or show business, something that I could focus on. I instinctively knew I didn't want to act in LA, and I wanted to do something to fit around the kids, so we bought an existing business from a groomer there. A few months later, we moved a few shops further up the road to a bigger premises next door to a vet. We catered for grooming, boarding and doggy day care. It was all very American, and extremely hard work. I used to start at 5.45am in the morning, and finish at 8pm at night, and worked there at least five days week. I ran that for almost a year, and despite inheriting some great staff, I was there pretty much every day for that whole period. Hard graft indeed. Our friend Jose Diaz, who is now a champion MMA fighter, also worked there when he was up-and-coming and training for fights.

Dogs have always played a massive part of my life since recovery. We always had a dog in our family home when I was growing up, usually Irish 'red' Setters, so I've not known life without dogs. I was always going to have dogs in my adult life, and once I had got clean and was married and finally settled with Kevin I made up for lost time yet again. I always wanted shorthaired dogs, like Dobermans, and I'm sure some people will hate on me for that. There's a stigma with 'Dobeys' and also Bullys (aka Bullmastiffs or Staffordshire Bull Terriers), my other preferred breeds. People talk about 'status' or 'council dogs', and I always say don't just judge the dog, judge the owner too.

At home in Essex we currently have my dog Rosie, a nine-month-old Bullmastiff, and Kevin's dog Alfie, a 'Staf', who is 18 months, and they are very much each our own dogs. I won't let Kevin tell my Rosie what to do. Oh no. I'm super protective of her. Despite being controversial, they're both great family dogs, stocky and fiercely loyal. Previously I've always had 'Dobeys', six of them in total at Gads Hill House. Most recently we had Della, or Del, and Rodney, who were half German / half British Dobermans. Del is huge and famously wrote off the front of a Ford Escort when she ran out in the road. She took it all in her stride...literally...got up, shook it off and trudged away like nothing had happened. We sent Del and Rodney away for police training for six weeks. They went straight from the breeders to the training camp, and we later worked out that you can't have dogs from the same litter, because they work in a pack. It's their instinct, and that's when it becomes dangerous. Eventually we had to split them up, and Del went to live with one of our friends.

Rodney has been all over the place with us...Spain, south of France and LA, and he's still out there in the States. We couldn't afford to bring him back, and I miss him terribly. He's only one month older than Jodie B, and like one of my kids. I'm hoping to have him back with us soon. Then there's Vinnie, who is an Argentinian Dogo cross blue-nosed Pitbull (the top two banned breeds in the UK). He's two years-old, and unable to travel into Europe. He's still out in LA as well, and lives with Jose Diaz.

Jodie's long-haired Pomeranian cross Chihuahua Lola Rouge, who was the boss of both Rodney and Vinnie, is also still in LA. She's such a minx, but we couldn't bring her back either, so for a while she went to stay with Sharon Osbourne and her numerous dogs. Lola is far too naughty, though, and kept beating up the Osbourne dogs so she is now with another friend in LA.

The Chihuahua aside, yes, these other dogs can be dangerous in the wrong hands, but if there is the correct discipline in the house then they are fine, and immensely loyal. A household without kids may have problems, if the dog assumes the role of the child, because then they will always be boss of that house. If there are kids in that house, and the dog appreciates the pecking order, then there shouldn't be any problems.

In Gad's I didn't ever put the alarms on. I had six 'Dobeys' protecting me, and I always said, if anyone can get past that little lot, then they're welcome to take what they want. During my recovery I've found dogs so comforting. It doesn't matter what mood you're in, it's pure unconditional love. You can scream and shout at them for walking mud through the house and they'll still look at you like a naughty child, as if to say: "I still love you." I went through long periods of my life when I had to make do with my own company...doing drugs for hours on end in isolation. Since my recovery I have also spent a lot of time hidden away, in my bedroom, and the dogs are great company.

Out in LA Barkingham Palace was perfect. We had the grooming parlour designed like a hair salon, so the dogs were sat on the grooming tables in front of massive ornate mirrors. The premises was four thousand square feet in total and open plan so everybody could see what was going on, including the dogs, who love to look around, as they're such sociable animals. On July 4th, Independence Day, there was a big demand to dye dogs red, white and blue, or green on St Patrick's Day. We were also asked to paint dog's toenails, or give them a mohawk...spike their hair up with gel. Very LA!

As for the dogs who were staying in our kennels, some of their owners were so eccentric, but then they do call their dogs out there "furry kids". Some would bring medication for them to take. One took antihistamines, for an allergy to pollen! Other owners would pack pyjamas for their dogs, or outfits for them to wear on specific days. We would be asked to text or email regular pictures of the dogs to some people, while others would ring up and speak to their dogs on the phone, from all corners of the world. We had anything up to 30 dogs boarding at one time.

We became good friends with a another couple in LA, Lili and Cleber Luciano. Lili brought her Maltese Terrier Daisy into the doggy parlour, and that's naturally how we met a lot of people out there. Brazilian Cleber is a famous champion MMA fighter. Neither he or Lili needed my fame, and that was great for our friendship. Kai has always wanted to do jiu jitsu so Cleber told us to bring him along to the gym he runs, and that was that, he was hooked. Their son Enzo hadn't been christened yet, but we became such good friends during the time we were in LA that we are now his godparents.

Lili and Cleber not knowing anything about our past, and in particular my colourful history, was a breath of fresh air. Lili once said to me: "So you're an actress. Why don't you act here? And, if I Google you, what will I find?...." I was, like: "Now, there's a story..." And because they are sports people, when they did Google me it was even more of a wow factor for them. But they didn't judge me and Lili said: "You did all that, and you're still alive... right, now you need to stop smoking."

As our stay in LA unfolded lots of people from the congregation at The Sanctuary started hanging around our shop. Then when people found out I was an actress with a colourful past I guess I was even more intriguing to them. Jay, our pastor, had been on American TV loads but in September 2011 I showed I could help spread The Sanctuary's word further afield, and straight across the Atlantic, live on ITV's *Lorraine* show.

Jay and I were sat in a studio in LA, and both chatted to Lorraine about my faith and The Sanctuary. I explained that, previously, I'd only ever been to church for weddings and funerals, and that nobody had ever told me about Jesus before. I admitted that attending The Sanctuary had helped Kevin and I also think about the way we treat people and the way we live our lives. Jay added: "It's amazing to watch the transformation that has happened with Danniella, and her family, and this is just the beginning." Lorraine said I looked great, which was lovely of her, and I did feel like I was in a very good space. However, all that was about to change, yet again.

(book launch photos, clockwise)
✧ With my good friend Cheryl, my brother 'Sarge' and mum
✧ Annie, Jodie, Kallum and Sam
✧ The amazing 'book cover' sweets supplied by VIP Events Essex
✧ DJ Jodie B

(book launch photos, clockwise) ✧ Jodie, Rose and Demi prepare for some photobooth action ✧ My old mates Brandon Block and Danny Dyer ✧ Me, Rita Simons and Cliff Paris, aka Minty, joking with the paps ✧ Catch's Nicky Hunt and wife Jackie

(book launch photos, clockwise) ✧ With my EastEnders mentor Jake Wood, and his wife Alison ✧ Me, Kevin and our long-time friend, comedian Ian Royce ✧ My dear friend Jody, who I named Jodie B after, and her beautiful daughter Amber

(book launch photos, clockwise)
✧ JamDeluxe and my mum
✧ Nanny Fluff and my cousin Laura ✧The amazing cup cakes made by Lou-Lou's Bakery

(book launch photos, clockwise) ✧ Kevin and his cousin Alan ✧ Photo-booth fun with Kevin, Danny Dyer, his wife Jo and Nicky Hunt ✧ Rita Simons and hubby Theo

(book launch photos, clockwise) ✧With my writer Matt, Catch owner Nicky Hunt, Brandon Block and Kevin ✧ Cliff Paris greets Jodie ✧ The wonderful Faith, Hope And Clarity cover cake by VIP Events Essex ✧ David Van Day and his wife Sue Moxley

15

TO LA AND BACK

Within a month of the appearance on *Lorraine* our LA adventure was over and we were heading back to the UK with a gloomy short-term future ahead. The same paper that had mocked my new faith ran a story about the impending closure of Barkingham Palace and over the last few weeks, after we made it known we were leaving, the majority of the members at the church backed off. Many people weren't supportive, and there was a lot of bickering and internal politics between the women there. You can't blame God for that, it's the individuals who need to look at themselves. Pastor Jay was very supportive and he and Christy have been to the UK to stay with us since we returned.

Sid Owen had been out to see us in LA very recently, with the hope of filming a reality show out there with me. He reckoned the dogs in Huntington Beach were TV gold alone. He was on the verge of potentially getting a series commissioned on it, but by then we were already on our way home. When we did return to the UK it was as the credit crunch continued to bite...on both sides of the pond.

We had simply run out of money. Kevin had started defaulting on his maintenance settlement to ex-wife Carol. These monthly payments were not an issue when Premier was at its prime, but like a lot of things, when the crunch hit, they started to hit us hard.

If Kevin didn't catch-up with those payments, Carol was technically entitled to half of the grooming shop. To stop this happening, Kevin would have to go back to the UK, leaving me and the kids in LA, and then deal with the courts. There was a chance he could have been imprisoned if things really didn't go in his favour. There was no way I could sit back in LA to wait and see what happened. We literally shut up shop, reluctantly dissolved Barkingham Palace and headed back to the UK. We were virtually broke because of all the money we'd invested into our new LA life. If we hadn't returned, there was also a chance Kevin would have been served a subpoena (or indicted) and that could mean he was never allowed back to the US again.

Back in Essex, we rented a house in the Great Dunmow area and, with a court case looming, Kevin sat at home for three weeks putting his defence together himself because we couldn't afford a lawyer. It was heartbreaking. I was fuming at the time, but Carol is entitled to what she's entitled too. Carol and I have had our ups and downs. and we haven't been that complimentary about each other over the years, but I have to say she's done a fantastic job bringing up her daughter. Jordan is a lovely young lady.

Divorces are never easy, and child support is always contentious. Fortunately the court could see that we had nothing left. Kevin told them: "If you want to put me away, I've got my bag packed here...do your worst." He wasn't being cocky, he'd just reached the end of his tether. Thankfully, it didn't come to that. Kevin came back to our small rented home that night, but was visibly distraught. We had no money, nothing left on our credit cards and no immediate prospects. Crash, bang, wallop! Back down to earth with a huge bump.

Our urgent return from LA in October 2011, the court case and our financial plight started to take its toll on all of us. It was now a case of "shit, we've got to pay the rent this month." I've never had to worry about that in my life, not even when I was a drug addict. We'd gone from Bentley and Porsche sending new cars to our mansion for us to test drive to scratching around to pay the bills for a rented two-bed house and driving a beaten up Ford Focus.

In our new home in a tiny village just outside Great Dunmow in Essex, Kai's room (or man cave) was a small office, and he slept on a sofa bed...it's a million miles away from the lap of luxury he had been used to, but a damn sight better than some of the places we lived in when I was at my addicted worst.

When we first moved things were extremely tight. Our lavish lifestyle had come to a humiliating end, and it was now a case of 'sell, sell, sell'. It was time to get rid of anything that could bring in some cash. Our Rolexes, my Chanel watch, Kevin's Breitling. My Louis Vuitton luggage went, although I didn't sell the Burberry stuff - they might be museum pieces one day! Loads of other designer handbags went. Just so we could get a deposit together and pay some rent in advance, and have some left over for bills and other running costs. No private schools for the kids now. It was the best local one we could find.

As we struggled and muddled through, my world was about to come tumbling down again for an altogether different reason. On Christmas Day, 2011, as I was taking a shower, I discovered four lumps on my right breast from the armpit down. I'd felt very achey on Christmas Eve around that area, but because of my extensive history of various boob jobs I didn't think much of it. But the next morning I checked again, and this time it seemed worse. I daren't say anything. It was Christmas Day, and I didn't want to spoil that. With limited funds we were trying to make the best we could of it anyway for the kids. Needless to say, it was eating away at me all day. My mum had cancer of the womb when I was 15, which she fortunately got through, but I remembered that she was the same sort of age then, as I was now. It was torture.

There had been a lot in the press about the PIP implants and hundreds of women were having those removed, but I knew I didn't have those so at least I wasn't worried on that front. For the next couple of days over the festive period it was agonising keeping it from Kevin, and I knew I wouldn't even be able to start making enquiries until at least the day after Boxing Day. I eventually told Kevin on the 28th, by blurting it out. I can't seem to keep anything from him for that long, especially if I'm asked what's wrong with me. I said to him: "Feel this and tell me what you think." He took one look and told me to get to the doctors immediately.

My first port of call, naturally was Jim Frame, who had performed the surgery for all my breast implants. His secretary apologised, explaining that he was too busy removing all the PIP implants. I was advised to head to my GP.

My closest girlfriend at the time had little sympathy for me, telling me in a brief phone call: "Chin up love, it's all going to be alright." She was so matter of fact, and dismissive, but I desperately needed another female to talk this through with. I wasn't speaking to my mum at the time, I'm not that close to my sister-in-law and my younger sister by my dad's second marriage is just too young. I needed a woman to speak too, and so I called Lili in America.

Lili's reaction couldn't have been more different. I had known her a fraction of the time, but suddenly she was offering to fly to London on the next plane to be with me while I waited for my appointment at the hospital.

She said her mum would come over from Brazil to look after her kids. No problem, she was on her way. I thought: "Wow, she's moving people all around the world for me." I appreciate everybody's circumstances are different, and Lili was able to offer that support. I've lost lots of friends along the way, often due to my own misgivings, but here was a new one showing such a good heart, and it didn't go unnoticed.

I headed to the village practice, during the week in between Christmas, and they referred me to Broomfield Hospital in Chelmsford. I had to wait three weeks, within which time I'd done a lot of research on the internet. I have to say the staff at Broomfield were absolutely brilliant. They have a special breast cancer unit there and were quickly able to confirm that the 'lumps' were inflamed glands and it was all stress related, which then all made perfect sense.

It was a huge relief, but a terrible strain at the time. Thankfully, at the age of almost 40 I was getting good news. There were women much younger than me at the hospital getting bad news. It was surreal, with us all in our gowns waiting for the thumbs up (or down!). Women aged in their '70s, right down to teenagers. My heart went out to all of them. I'd been clean so long I took my health for granted, and never even thought about getting regular checks. When you're using you just don't care about your health. It's a roll of the dice whether you wake up the next morning.

I may have survived this scare, but Kevin and I were struggling personally again. My bipolar disorder was raging, and something was always going to give. Neither of us were working, the lumps in my breasts had scared the hell out of me and Kevin and I were at each other's throats every day. One argument on a Sunday spilled over. It was nasty, like we hated each other. Kevin came running in the lounge in tears. "You don't know how much I've loved you. I've never been so low." He threw his mobile phone down on the sofa, and said: "I won't be needing this." He then went and scrambled around in the medicine cabinet in the bathroom. When he reappeared he looked broken, and added: "I just don't know how long I can go on like this," and stormed out of the house. I was petrified, but also knew he needed some space and time to think things through. We had some friends who had an empty house in the next village, which Kevin had been helping decorate. He had a set of keys so I hoped he'd be there...and I was right.

I was trying to keep my composure, because Jodie was crying, over what she had heard Kevin say, or as I tried to stress, what she thought she had heard Kevin say. Kai wanted to jump on his bike and chase after him, but I insisted he stay where he was. I carried on regardless with the roast dinner I was cooking, and started to prepare the kids' school uniforms and PE kits for the morning. I then packed Kevin a bag, with his laptop and a few other bits in it, and drove to the house where he was. I posted his phone through the letter box, and texted him a message saying I would leave him be for a couple of days and left the bag and his dinner in the porch. Then it was a case of hoping for the best. I didn't think at this stage that bashing on the door and continuing the row was going to help the situation.

The thing with Kevin is that he just doesn't do half-empty. He's always full, or at the very worst half-full. That's why I've always thought he is further down the road with his faith than me. He always says his faith is around 75 per cent and mine is about 30-35 per cent. At that precise moment I had to believe that his faith was strong enough to pull him through, whatever the stats were. When I got home I couldn't help myself, so I phoned Kevin to tell him his dinner was outside. He didn't pick-up so I started to panic. I rang my friends and asked if they would go round and check on him. They rushed round there, but Kevin wouldn't come to the door. They let themselves in and there he was, sprawled out on the sofa.

Kevin had left our house and walked six miles in total through the country lanes that led to our friend's place. He had bought a bottle of vodka from the first village store he came to and says he rowed with God the whole way there. It was as if the last 13 years of his life had turned up all at once. Kevin had no cash to buy me or himself out of this one. He couldn't jet off to the south of France to see his therapist, or book into his favourite central London hotel. There was no retail therapy to cover up the cracks of this one. He couldn't hear what I was saying, how much I was moaning. He felt he had spent so long dealing with the trouble and strife of my life that he had literally no time for his own. He says eventually God came knocking and asked: "What about you?"

At his self-styled retreat Kevin swallowed a handful of the painkillers and ran himself a bath, but didn't touch the vodka. He says he continued to bicker with the big man upstairs during his soak, insisting he was ready to take control of our lives again, and then crashed out on the sofa, more spun out on the painkillers than anything else. He claims he was happily reading his bible when the 'rescue crew' arrived. Yes, he was buzzing a bit, but he assured them he was fine.

It was like Kevin was completely worn out by the climatic finale of the last few months...the court case, my medical scare and the general struggle of every day. And we were struggling. Sometimes we didn't even have a tenner to put petrol in the car. It was a terrible personal burden on such a proud man.

Our friends insisted on taking Kevin to hospital because they were worried he had taken too many painkillers, and he reluctantly went with them. By now I was fuming, and left them all to it. Like when a child goes missing, and you're so relieved they've been found that now you're furious they put you through it all, I had the audacity to think of myself once more. I was furious.

What if Kai had gone round there on his bike and found Kevin like that. It would have haunted him forever. Now it was my time to have a drink, and I sat there with two friends from the village drowning my own sorrows for a bit, while Kevin was given the once over at Chelmsford Hospital.

He had gone willingly, and was discharged at 4am, but didn't come home. He went and stayed back at our friends house...for a total of three months. It was a breakdown, plain and simple, and hardly surprising. Of course, I felt terrible, at the various parts I had played along the way. And I was in bits too. Jodie was in tears every day. We'd left our dream lifestyle in LA, and even our dogs, because we simply hadn't been able to afford to bring them back. And Kevin, everybody's rock, was rock bottom. But I didn't want him back...yet. We loved each other, but we hated each other too. I think I needed to reach rock bottom again as well, to flush out the gluttony of my materialistic decade of being clean, once and for all. I knew it also meant I desperately needed confirmation, finally, that I was on the bipolar spectrum.

In the short term, If I didn't get on top of the rent quickly, myself and the kids were heading for a hostel again. The first time for Jodie B, but not for me and Kai. So I went online and applied for housing benefit and child maintenance. I went to the job centre in Braintree and signed on. I had no option. How that little trip didn't make the papers, I'm not quite sure. Every other major turning point in my life had been splashed all over the tabloids, but maybe God was looking down on me, as I shuffled along the dole queue that day. But I'm not proud. I don't care what people think. I had to do it to support my children...our children. My husband was mentally and physically worn out. I had no option, and I am so thankful that I was eligible for those payments. They helped me put life in perspective like never before. They may have brought me crashing back down to earth, but they also gave me a grounding, and a great platform from which to build from.

I'm genuinely so grateful that it happened to us. It taught me so much about economising...largely thanks to Asda, I might add. And, while we're at it, let's also give a big shout out to the 99p Store. Kai's school dinner was costing £4.00 a day so I scrapped that, and it was packed lunches from then on. I mean, £2.50 for a panini? Really? Kai's used to a big breakfast, but as long as I made sure there was plenty of bread and chocolate spread in stock he was OK.

I would hate to sound patronising, but I appreciate that for many people Asda and the likes of Poundland, and budgeting with school dinners, are the norm, not rock bottom. Everyone has their rock bottom, though, and I'd spectacularly reached mine. This time it wasn't through drugs and drinking it was through being too materialistic and the general pressures of life, relationships and a crippling credit crunch which hit everyone hard. I know, better than most, that you're only ever as strong as the situations you find yourself in. We all have to cut our cloth accordingly at times, and it was now time for me to batten down the hatches and be strong for the kids.

With my husband getting the space he so badly needed, I reluctantly headed to my village GP. to talk to them about bipolar disorder. Thankfully the mental health team assigned to that surgery were able to help. After trying so hard to shake my reputation as a cocaine addict, I didn't want the stigma of bipolar. I couldn't bear to be labelled again. Deep down I knew I had it, I just didn't want to admit that, like so many things in my life.

A few weeks before we left LA, as our return became more and more likely, I visited the medical centre where I was registerred locally. The doctor was running late and by the time she saw me explained that she didn't have a lot of time because she needed to pick her daughter up from ballet. She literally asked me what I wanted. I said: "Xanax please." This is a drug which treats anxiety and panic attacks, but the doctor didn't ask me about any symptoms, whether I was having any panic attacks...just gave me the Xanax there and then. I was in and out within two minutes. There is such a liberal attitude to medication in LA. They also have something called the Medical Marijuana Card, which allows people to smoke and possess a certain amount of cannabis. Loads of people seem to have them.

Out there people exchange 'meds' like kids swapping marbles in a playground, and so many of our friends, including those at the church, did so too. The doctors hand them out like 'well done' stickers at school. Each day I was taking up to four or five of the sleeping tablets, and at least three Xanax, which is now banned in the UK. Towards the end of our stay in the States symptoms of bipolar disorder were overpowering.

When we did return in the autumn of 2011 I had enough meds to get me through October and November, but then ran out. I couldn't get any Xanax, and so tried to do 'cold turkey' through until May. By that time Kevin had left. I had hit rock bottom, personally, financially and mentally. That's when I gave in, and went to see my GP. He had to do something drastic, so I was initially prescribed six to nine 25mg of the sedative Temazepam a day and a 200mg anti-depressant called Mirtazapine, renowned for weight gain, and that quickly saw me pile on the pounds, almost three stones in total. Fortunately, I was able to reduce that dosage dramatically over the next few months and (eventually) lose most of the weight too.

The medication side of bipolar is a constant worry to me. Forever concerned about becoming addicted to these drugs, I refuse to self-medicate. If I don't think what I'm prescribed is strong enough I will never take any more until I speak to my GP, and even then he'll probably only tell me to take an extra half a tablet for a couple of days. Because I am a drug addict, if I start increasing my own dosage drastically, like I used to without a care in the world with cocaine, then I may as well give up and go out and get some some crack. I know that sounds extreme, but drug addiction is extreme, and that's how strongly I now feel about it.

As much as I have struggled with bipolar disorder, it's as if a little bit of me does enjoy sitting in it. Now, I know I need to own it, that I must go to the doctor and get more meds if I run out, and that I must try and talk things through.

This was no time for therapists, and there was simply no way we could afford that luxury anymore. A psychiatric nurse at the hospital who had seen Kevin suggested we got some marriage guidance, but we were both well past all that. With our house being so small I knew Kevin badly needed the space he was getting. I had my budget to work from and I was keeping a roof over the rest of us, and not before time either.

After that initial 24-48 hours of Kevin being away, when he had come back from the hospital, the kids got to see him every day. We were apart for a total of three months, but the split eventually came to a natural end. Kevin stayed over at our house one night, and I said: "Well, you can't stay at the other place forever." Kevin asked me what I wanted and I told him: "We want you to come home. We've got a routine now. I've changed. We've all changed."

I've lost count of the times we've split up, but no relationship is easy. After the extravagance of the Gads Hill House era, and the ups and down since, I am prepared, more than ever, to go out and work, and give something back to the relationship. Those three months were definitely the lowest I've been outside of addiction, as I'm sure it was for Kevin too.

DANNIELLA WESTBROOK

16
TIME TO TELL ALL

With Kevin back in the fold, as we approached Christmas 2012 and I started to write this book, I finally found the courage to talk about the pivotal moment in my life. This was no time for half-a-story, or skimming around the edges. No more self-denial.

It dates back to the mid '90s, a time when the more people tried to make me stop taking cocaine, the more coke I did. I moved to south London in 1994 at the age of 21 to get away from Essex and my family. I'd lost connection with them, and my friends in Chigwell. They didn't want to hang out with anyone from south London, to slum it down there. They wanted to glam up and go to Epping Forest Country Club. They were still all about champagne and vodka, lime and sodas. I was so wrapped up in cocaine, so addicted.

Based in a nice apartment block in Tower Bridge, I lived with a friend of mine, a dancer, who was away a lot. It was only a one bed flat, because we couldn't afford anywhere bigger. We shared the bedroom...not that I slept that much.

I suppose I got a buzz out of south London. I loved the danger, absolutely got off on it. Loughton was just too safe for me. I grew up in a nice house there, but it just wasn't as edgy in Essex. I rebelled against the 2.4 kids thing and turned my back on those leafy suburbs. I'd grown up there, but I found it boring and fake.

The south London I knew was like a Martina Cole book. It was raw, murky and edgy, and I guess if you lay down with dogs you'll eventually get fleas. I'd seen some extreme violence in the short time I'd lived in south London.

In the mid-90s it was almost as if I became my *EastEnders* character, Sam Mitchell. She was always a rebel and with Phil and Grant there was always that criminal element to her life. When I got to south London it was as if I'd left Loughton, stopped off at Albert Square in east London and then headed down to Bermondsey via the Blackwall Tunnel. It somehow felt like home and the most appropriate place to settle.

I quickly got in deep with loads of dealers in the area, and within months owed them silly amounts of money. Of course, the person that you owe the money to, owes it to someone else. One morning there was a knock on the door at my flat on the borders of Bermondsey. The three guys standing there were polite and said they had come about a dealer I was in with for about five grand, explaining that the debt had now been passed up to them. The dealer in question used a nickname, which I can't even remember properly now, as I was getting gear from so many different people at that time. I asked them in knowing I had little choice.

Three guys, all white and wearing Stone Island, were pleasant enough at the start, but when I told them I didn't have the money, or access to it, the atmosphere changed. I caught the odd look at their faces when I dared, but otherwise kept my head down, frantically smoking, desperately trying to think of a way out of this mess.

I had my back to them, as I made cups of tea, and grimaced as the mood continued to get darker.

"You must have a family member who can loan you the money. Or your agent? Someone you work with? We can drive you there now."

There was no easy way out. I was bang in trouble. I assured them I had fallen out with my parents, that they'd moved away and I'd lost touch. How could I appear on their doorstep with these lads demanding that sort of cash.

"What about your brother?," they asked.

"He's still at school," I explained.

They weren't taking 'no' for an answer and kept saying the debt had been passed over, and they couldn't leave until something was sorted. But I was skint. Brassic. Driving in neutral if I could. That broke! The only thing I could get any credit on was coke.

It was mid-morning, around 11am. As usual, I'd been up most of the night and I was still in my dressing gown.

One of them told me to get dressed, and explained that I was going with them.

"Shit!"

I readily assumed I would be beaten and dumped somewhere. It wasn't rocket science. Thoughts were racing through my fragile mind. I'm going to end up in hospital. Just how low have I gone?

Within minutes I had changed into a tracksuit and was sat in a BMW, probably a Three Series, driving further south, possibly through Kennington, over to Vauxhall and down to Stockwell. But I can't be sure. A mixture of fear, sleep deprivation and that awful wired feeling from severe coke addiction had left me desperate and disorientated. "Fuck, fuck, fuck," I said to myself as we pulled up at another traffic light. "Where's a police car when you need one?," I wondered. Not that jumping out and banging on its window would do me any favours. Or that I wanted to involve the Old Bill anyway. Causing a commotion or waving my arms frantically wasn't going to wash with this lot. There would only be further repercussions. This lot were not frightened of the police, or anyone, for that matter.

"Right, what pubs do you use?...let's check them out, see if there's anyone there who can help you...," one said, upping the ante.

"I don't use pubs," I protested. "Honestly...I'm at home all the time."

Something I said worked. But not necessarily in my favour. We pulled up in a side street. I was ordered out of the car, shuffled 50-odd yards towards one property and ushered up the ten or eleven front steps of a typical victorian house and quickly led into the ground floor flat.

However, this was no crack house. Unfortunately I knew the difference. It was tastefully furnished, but there were no family photos anywhere. And no landline phone. One of them offered me a drink. "Some vodka?," I thought. "Why not?" I could certainly do with a drink after what I'd been through that morning. And a "big line of gear?" You bet. I really need one of those.

The guys were sniffing coke and making calls on their large mobile phones. While they waited for instructions of what to do next, they became increasingly aggressive with every line and drink. I accepted more coke from them, and more vodka. Anything to try and help black out and numb the fear of what was possibly about to happen.

"Right, then," one slurred ominously, after what seemed like hours. "It's down to us then. You're going to have to pay the debt somehow. You'll have to do what we say. Your little actress thing isn't going to work anymore."

They had exhausted all options on the phone and were hardly in any condition to negotiate had they found someone to bail me out. They hadn't let me bring my mobile with me when we left my flat, but I was sure people would be ringing...friends, other dealers. My car was also there. I couldn't be away forever. I couldn't be here forever. My absence would be noticed. They themselves couldn't disappear for that long. All these thoughts gave me hope.

I'd completely lost track of time. The blinds had been firmly shut since we arrived, four...or possibly six...God knows...maybe eight hours earlier. I'd had countless large vodkas by now, loads of gear and a couple of pills, which I assumed were Ecstasy tablets. From minute to minute, hour to hour I did what I thought was needed to get through this hell. I tried to remain as upbeat as physically possible, but this seemed to be heading in only one direction.

I couldn't scream. I couldn't kick-off or try and escape. I drifted in and out of consciousness, but when I came round they were always there, staring at me, digging at me, plying me with more booze and more lines. I now struggled to work out where I was, strained to hear what they were talking about. If I went to the toilet they told me to leave the door open. It all made the paranoia worse. I must have been there at least 24 hours by now.

What exactly were they going to do to me? These guys were in a different league and didn't play by the rules. These weren't old school bank robbers enjoying their retirements in Marbella. Nor were they dealers from the local estate. But I wasn't breaking. There were no hysterics. I did owe them money, and because they hadn't beaten me up I thought I could muddle through this living nightmare, that drinking and sniffing with them would gloss over the whole thing. I prayed eventually they'd get bored, order me a cab and send me home. Until I was taken through to the bedroom for the first time. Alone with one of them. With the door shut.

As much as I have blocked out so much of my life, I am simply unable to forget what happened next. I knew what he was doing to me. I knew what they all did to me. I know all three of them did different things. Repeatedly. They all forced themselves on me. They all raped me, and took it in turns. Several times over the next 24-36 hours. However long it took for them to feel my debt had been paid. For them a two-day drugs and sex binge. For me a lifetime sentence. Each time I laid there and let them get on with it. I tried to mask it out, tried to pass out. There was no point resisting. Not with three of them. And they knew what they were doing. They were clever and didn't mark me or beat me up. They knew the wrong people would have asked the right questions. Then when they were finished with me they turfed me out of the flat. Broken and empty.

I roamed the streets, sobbing - a household name with my head down and the game up. Trying to fight back the tears, I sniffled and shuffled in what I thought was the right direction. I can't tell you where I had been holed up or what these thugs looked like. I systematically erased their faces and that flat from my memory on that desperate journey home. With no money to hail a cab or a phone to ring a friend I staggered back, numb and ashamed. It was daylight, mid afternoon, that I can remember. It wasn't either hot or cold. It wasn't Christmas. It must have been Spring or Autumn. I felt my way home like the south London street rat I had become. Scouring the area for drugs on a regular basis meant an in-built sat-nav immediately kicked in. My experience as a wide-eyed clubber trawling from party to party did me proud. But that's where any pride stopped. I'd ruined my career, lost my family and now this. I was sure the only way to cope was to forget about it. I told myself I deserved my ordeal. That it was a fitting punishment for all the pain I had caused others. Finally indoors, I drew every curtain and closed every blind. I hoped I could shut out the pain. I ran a bath, and washed my hair. More baths, more rinses, again and again and again. Desperate to wash away the stench and stain of what happened and what I had become.

I stayed at home for three days. Nothing new there, but for the first time in ages I didn't use. I just drank wine. I hadn't gone three days without cocaine since I could remember. This was the cleanest I'd been in years, yet I felt so dirty and disgusting. So helpless and horrified. Disturbed and distraught. I told nobody...absolutely no-one. My parents had divorced. I couldn't ring them, it would have broken their hearts. Dad is a carpet fitter, bless him, not a villain. What could he have done? He could have hardly gone looking for them. I'd already been the biggest pain in the arse possible.

I couldn't bring myself to go to the police...I just couldn't. Then something somewhere made me snap out of it a day or two later, and I took myself to the doctors to get an AIDs test, and to be checked out for any other sexually transmitted diseases. A week later I got the all clear, a massive boost which helped me try to gradually get on with my life again. Except I couldn't see past cocaine. It had got me to this place, and now I reasoned it could bloody well try and help me deal with its own horrific consequences. I was using again within days, and my usual large amounts within a week. Getting coke on credit still not an issue, but had I not learned any lessons?

I had to drag myself out of this anguish somehow, and get on with life. Get on with taking as much coke as I could to block out the trauma. And so I did. I banged away at the gear and pretty much buried the most horrific 48 hours of my life for the next two decades.

During this period, like so many in my life, I seemed to lurch from one drama to another. I had to battle on through somehow after the trauma of my 'abduction'. I did that, the only way I knew...by taking extreme amounts of cocaine. A warped case of "the show must go on".

One day I met up for a drink with an old friend of mine, a girl I had taken drugs with regularly over the years. We ended up back at her place, finishing off what gear we both had. When it had all gone, she lost it, insisting we drive around looking for some more.

Eventually I managed to get bail on an eighth of an ounce, so roughly three and a half grams on tick.

With us two in full flow, an eighth was hardly going to touch the sides. My 'friend' drove for another 45 minutes or so, and we somehow ended up in a grubby caravan on a camping site somewhere in the middle of nowhere. God's knows why or where, or whose it was? I have no idea, it was so random. I just remember the grotty interior of this moody caravan, an old portable TV flickering away in the background and heavy rain pouring down on the roof as we pounded away at the coke. Within two hours we'd done the lot, and now my pal was really flipping out. She grabbed me and literally threw me out of the caravan and into the car again. We were back on the road, and in search of more gear. I was scared now, but needed coke too.

This was clearly as far from the recreational side of drugs as you could get. You wouldn't even go out in this kind of downpour in the early hours, let alone drive hopelessly around south London housing estates looking for cocaine. This mad woman had me knocking on dealers' doors at 5am, marching me up their paths, with my arm behind my back, so I could beg for more cocaine. Understandably nobody would answer their door. At one set of traffic lights she punched me full in the face as we argued, cutting my nose and splitting my lip open. With blood seeping from my wounds, I desperately tried to pull myself together and somehow managed to get some kind of grip on the situation. I was still in an extremely bad place from the events of a couple of weeks before, but I reasoned that, comparatively, this was a walk in the park.

I told this nutcase to drive to another friend's house, that she would have some coke. This pal was actually as straight as they come. She never touched drugs, but could handle herself, and always looked out for me. When we pulled up, I sprinted from the car and banged on the windows, screaming for help. My friend and her mum opened the front door and found me, blood pouring from my facial wound, with this mad woman chasing me up their path. Thankfully, they put her in her place, and threatened to call the police if she didn't leave, which certainly had the desired effect.

This incident was the final straw for me. After sleeping at my friend's place, I sheepishly headed back to my mum's in Loughton, as I did from time to time, vowing to get clean. Typically, I'd rest up there, eat well, and have genuine intentions of going back to south London, to clear my flat out, and move back to my mum's. However, I'd be back to my old ways in my old haunts within a matter of days. After the torment of my rape ordeal, you would think south London was the last place I'd want to be, but it had such a desperate hold on me.

I've always had control issues, and struggle if I'm told to do something. If someone told me I was making good progress with my recovery, and that getting clean was the right thing to do, I would automatically rebel against that. Once again, I would get my mum's hopes up. My sleeping patterns would improve. I looked and felt healthier, but all the time I was clucking for coke. Just when she'd thought she'd got me back, I was off again, back on the road to destruction.

17
HOPE

Almost 20 years later, I had still only told one person what those guys did to me, and it wasn't Kevin. He'd been told a comparatively innocent version, that some lads had made me do coke and pills with them because I owed their mate money. My biggest fear was that if I told Kevin the whole story, he'd leave me. And it was a whole five years after those assaults that I even got together with Kevin.

The one person who did know was Beechy Colclough. When you're in treatment, it's common to be told you're holding something back. They can tell. And I always have been. With every therapist I've seen I've known it's impossible for them to get to the root of my problems without knowing what happened back then. And I was fine with that. If they couldn't get it out of me, then I was happy to leave it where it was. Before Beechy I hadn't connected with any therapist well enough to talk about the assault, but then I thought I did know Beechy well enough. I felt comfortable delving back into it all. But even then I couldn't reveal the whole ordeal to him. Then when I felt Beechy betrayed me, I buried it even more.

It has been hard living with so many of my mistakes, especially the guilt of using coke when I was pregnant with Kai, but despite the fact that I couldn't stop using coke in the mid-90s, it was so important for me to have Kai. I just wanted someone who would be there for me...unconditionally. And that may be selfish, and I may have risked Kai's health because of that, but that's the way it is. I've taken so much stick for using cocaine throughout that pregnancy, and deservedly so, but, if at all possible, I want people to try and understand why I was still using cocaine before, during and after Kai's birth.

Many will say that you can't condone my actions whatever had happened in my past. All I can say is that now that I've had all this time to process it, I know why I was still taking cocaine during labour several years after the assault. Kai was something to cling on to, something that gave me hope of some kind of normality in the future. Something to try and build on. The post traumatic stress I was sub-consciously suffering from the assault was just too severe to deal without cocaine. I wish I could have been stronger, but I just didn't have it in me, and for that I have hated myself ever since.

After the assaults I just felt so worthless. Why did nobody come and get me? Did nobody care enough? Was I that unlovable? All irrational thoughts that rushed in and out of my mind. I didn't feel like anyone did care enough, until I met Kevin, but it was still so hard to say exactly what happened.

Kevin was the real deal. For the first time since the assault I felt safe. I fell in love with him immediately. Besotted with me, I knew he wouldn't let me come to harm. I was knocked off my feet that he wanted to be with me. It was such a relief when I met him. Kevin loving me and caring about me felt wonderful. It wasn't really the money. It was the simple things. Making sure I had something to eat. Just the sheer companionship was a godsend. It was so refreshing that Kevin didn't want anything from me. Up until then I'd only been with people who had bled me dry. It was as if I had been waiting for Kevin all my life.

However, both Kevin and I clearly had a distorted view of life. I was bang on the coke still, and his life was like the Ray Winstone film Love, Honour and Obey. When I met Kevin he was running around town, drinking heavily and taking lots of Ecstasy. Within weeks I was driving a Porsche feeling like I had the keys to the city. We should have been a disaster, but somehow it worked. It took us years to sort ourselves out and amazingly we survived as a couple to tell the tale.

Kevin reckons that first chance meeting was God fighting fire with fire, years before we discovered our faith. Kevin was the first person I'd been out with who didn't want to sleep with me immediately. He moved me and Kai in to his luxury apartment, and said: "You two can sleep in the spare room." He wasn't trying to take advantage of me. He wasn't trying to own me. He had fallen in love with me. It was a huge experience.

On the flip side, the assault had a hugely detrimental affect on our relationship. It's been hard for me to connect romantically and sexually. I did with Kevin at the start, but, if I'm honest, ever since I was unceremoniously sent packing from that flat in south London I've found it hard to love anyone, including myself. Years later, even when my kids cuddled me I went stiff. I couldn't feel that whole maternal love thing for a long time. The things those guys did to me has left me feeling violated ever since. I couldn't tell Kevin. I didn't want him to think I was some old slapper. I tried to broach the subject when I made my *Ghost Towns* confession, but the timing wasn't right. What I did tell him was so watered down. I didn't tell him they frightened me, let alone touched me.

Kevin deserved better, but it never seemed the right time to tell him. It wasn't like I could go out and get another guy like him, but I always felt he could have bettered himself. Instead, every time we broke up he always came back to me. It's taken years of him being extremely understanding, but it has tainted the whole time I've been with him. I've hated myself so much. Sexually and mentally I switched off. Because of my guilt, I couldn't get in the right headspace. I thought I was betraying Kevin because he didn't know, but equally I thought he wouldn't want to be with me if he found out. I knew I was a laughing stock about drugs, so assumed no-one would believe me if I did reveal what I'd gone through. I'm sure a lot of people still don't.

If my drink had been spiked and I ended up in that flat with those guys doing what they did, I think it would have been different. I wouldn't have felt it was my fault. Who knows what was in those pills. They could have been Rohypnol. I don't know. Whatever the case, it was my drug addiction that got me in that situation, so I did blame myself. So many nights me and Kevin have sat up in bed arguing. I'd say: "I can't tell you why I don't feel attractive, why I won't sleep with you." Some things you just think you'll take to your grave.

We've split up so many times in the last 14 years, but are now together forever. It even held me back when I became a Christian. I couldn't believe I would be accepted into any church? Just how much shit can you be forgiven for? Does God really feel like I'm worth saving? I was looking at Kevin developing his faith a lot quicker, and wondering why he was so far ahead of me. Now I've finally spoken about this I feel much more comfortable spiritually too.

When I started thinking about this second book, and started working on it, deep down I knew this issue needed to be addressed. It's held the whole of our marriage back, and the way I have parented, but now I've talked about it I feel like I can finally work through it. I was so frightened about being labelled again, but now I feel like I've stripped myself as bare as I possibly can.

I realise that I'm not alone either. There are many women, who have been raped and haven't been able to talk about it for various reasons. From time to time I do voluntary work at the Pillion Trust homeless shelter in London. Some horrible things happen to the people who seek comfort there. So many people still think the streets are paved with gold, when for lots they're full of misery. I still believe that my drug addiction meant I was in that wholly vulnerable situation, and also appreciate that lots of women are victims of domestic rape. I understand that a wife at home, who feels she can't risk the break up of her own family, may turn to drink or even drugs to mask what is going on behind closed doors. Talking about my own situation helped me complete my own horrific journey. And by speaking out I hope others will find the strength to do so. Life is too short to have trauma like that bottled up inside.

Maybe my ordeal explains why, in my drug-addled state, I seriously thought about becoming an escort, or wanted Kevin beaten up. Why not? It surely couldn't be any worse than what I'd already been through. If Kevin didn't want me anymore, then, yeah, let's rough him up a bit... "If I can't have him, nobody can". What use would he be to me if he wasn't there looking after me? That whole episode on coast was ludicrous. Kevin was and is the only man who makes me feel safe. Now he had left me, somehow I was able to be so harsh. It's just so crazy now, looking back. Hopefully it shows that in the middle of addiction, in the depths of psychosis, that it is possible to change. If just one other person faces up to their fears and steers their life back in the right direction then me speaking out will have been worthwhile.

In the days, months and years after my rape ordeal cocaine helped me block everything out as much as possible. I've never been as confident since. But however much coke I took it was never enough to wash it all away. I'll never totally lose the memory of those 48 hours. It's always there. We've all got skeletons, but I can be driving along with the kids, and it will pop into my head. The other day I was watching a BBC TV drama, and a scene came on where a girl was being raped. I was watching with Kai...and instinctively fast-forwarded it. Kai was like: "Mum, it's not real, chill out." What could I say? If I watch anything like that, Jodie Foster on the pool table in The Accused, or something else similar, my chest tightens and everything I've tried to numb comes rushing back.

As the years have passed, and even more so now I've got it out in the open, I've learned to believe that I have nothing to be ashamed of. It's all part of one big mistake...it's the harsh reality of drugs. It doesn't matter who or where you are, if you're not careful, drugs can be one big rocky road. It may start in a nightclub, but it can be far from glamorous when you're done with it, or more like, it's done with you. I've had to pull myself together, and it's time to get it out there, and time for someone else to own it. If the people who raped me are somehow reminded of it, then, great, let them deal with it too.

Maybe that whole ordeal would have panned out differently today, with smart phones. It's possible there would have been photos and video footage of the early few hours at the flat, and, I don't know, perhaps it wouldn't have gone as far as it did because of that, or, worse ways, it would have been made public somehow and the guys would have been caught. It would have been gruesome to deal with like that, but it may have ended my torment 17, 18, 19 years earlier.

I still wonder whether the person at the top of the tree had any idea of what went on. Within two weeks, the guy I got the drugs from in Greenwich, who I owed the five grand, had moved. Nobody heard from him again. Not that I can remember his name. Even what he looks like is a big blur now. Surely, the guilt I've felt over the years is nothing compared to what those guys feel like. Well, hopefully anyway. You know, I forgive them. I've had to move on. They're out there somewhere, maybe they've got their own kids and families. Let them own it.

Getting all this shit out has enabled me to try and move on. In fact, Kevin reckons that when I confessed to the wrap party fling, and started to talk about the drug debt assaults, it was the first time since he'd known me that I started to be honest. It's been torture carrying everything for so long. I've tried to deal with things daily, and not dwell on it. When you do manage to put the drugs down you're left with all the mental stuff... the terrible bi-products of the addiction, and to deal with all the things that you've previously tried to forget. It was why I could go on *The Jeremy Kyle Show* and talk about using cocaine during the pregnancy. I finally knew why I had done that. Why I allowed that to happen. I started out with a carrier bag of guilt and ended up with the full Louis Vuitton luggage set. I'd say I'm back down to a small vanity case now. And for the most part, I think I've put most of my guilt in a black bin bag, and thrown it out with the trash.

DANNIELLA WESTBROOK

18
THE BI-PRODUCT

As sad as it was to leave, LA was not the best place for me to finally get on top of bipolar. Sure, it was there I started to understand it better, but with prescription drugs so freely available in the States I believe it was better treated back in the UK.

Previously I fought against the medication I was given for depression, but I understand more about bipolar now, and have got past the name. Ideally, I don't want to be taking any tablets, because I don't want to become addicted to them, but if it works and I can still be in control and earn a living, then so be it. After what I saw in LA, where so many people are addicted to prescription drugs and self-prescribing is such a huge problem, then I'm always going to be mindful of my situation. It's a crazy place. Out there even dogs have therapists.

However, by talking to doctors in LA I was able to step back and see the grip it had on me. It was in the States, in treatment in Arizona, where I was first diagnosed with bipolar disorder. I found out more about it in Huntington Beach, but it wasn't until 2012 back in Essex that I got it under control.

Many think bipolar disorder is a posh term for manic depression, but that's generalising it far too much. It can be common in those suffering with extensive drug and alcohol addiction, like me, when the serotonin levels in your brain have taken a battering over the years, but it's much more complex than that. You start obsessing about things that aren't that important, and take other much more dramatic events in your stride. At times you can feel the blood in your body boiling. If not treated properly, you're either really hyped or really low.

At times Kevin is like my live-in therapist. He says that when my bipolar disorder kicks in, it's as if I don't like him...like I don't love him, never did and never will. He says, for a husband or partner, if not treated or understood, living with someone on the bipolar spectrum can be like banging your head against a brick wall...like he can't breathe. It's sometimes so overpowering he thinks he is the person who is ill. He reckons treating someone with cancer or a loss of a limb, for example is, if anything, much more transparent, because you can see that illness.

When business was good and money wasn't an issue, Kevin would try to buy me out of bipolar, and that worked for almost a decade and cost a huge amount of money. Then when the cash ran out and we were on our knees, when I couldn't use retail therapy or didn't have enough money to go to lunch with my friends, I took myself to the doctors and a handful of tablets on a prescription costing a fiver was able to get on top of it.

I believe it was God's way of taking everything away from me, so that I could get well. In fact, I believe we've both lost so much, so we could both get well. We are literally here but for the grace of God. Deep down, I like to think our's is a good old fashioned love story...love has to be the only reason we're still together.

I am now on top of bipolar disorder. I know I need to try and move on from certain deep-rooted issues in my past. We all do, and that's the difficult bit. That's what can suddenly send you tumbling back into depression. It's easier said than done, of course, but if you spend too much time looking back you'll surely miss new opportunities coming through.

The tricky part of controlling bipolar disorder is that I need to take my meds. Working closely with a doctor is crucial.

When my bipolar is at its worst and untreated I can literally sleep at the drop of a hat. I can drift in and out of consciousness with ease. It's like I go into auto-pilot and shutting myself away from the world seems the most natural thing. It's so hard to get out of that headspace. Eventually, something clicks and I'm back in the room, but it can take days. Without my medication, anything can trigger a return to a more rational way of thinking, or sometimes I find the strength to dig myself out of it.

In the depths of the bipolar spectrum I literally feel like the walking dead. There must be hundreds of thousands of people sloping or bouncing around not knowing they've even got it. If I put on my bipolar cap I can dip in and out. I know there are times I've used it to my advantage, and that the whole thing can be self-perpetuating. At its worst, in the space of ten minutes, I can change from a happy-go-lucky person, to someone dejected and downtrodden. I can deal with all kinds of drama easily, then flip out to the simplest of things. It rubs off on everyone around you too - your partner and the kids. For one reason or another I've lived for so many years ignoring bipolar disorder but, like an athlete with a torn muscle, if not treated I'll never be able to perform or compete properly.

I certainly don't miss the extreme paranoia and continual comedowns that my extensive use of cocaine ensured, but when my bipolar is in full effect, or I've run out of meds, it can be equally as debilitating as hard drugs themselves. Again, I can safely say that if giving up cocaine was the easy bit then living with the aftermath can still be torturous. Any happy memories I have of being on cocaine slip further into the past the more the depression eats away...the more I beat myself up for the poor choices I have made over the course of my life. At its worst bipolar can be as crippling as cold turkey. And while I was able to give up coke more than 12 years ago, giving up bipolar disorder is not an option. It nullifies you just like any extreme addiction can, except you're not addicted to it...it's addicted to you.

There is simply no physiological test to confirm the disorder, so when diagnosing bipolar disorder it's very difficult to distinguish it from depression in general. One school of thought is that 'major life events' - both good or bad - can trigger the disorder, and that clearly ticks plenty of boxes where I'm concerned. When bipolar was discussed at Cottonwood, I was so happy I was now giving up cocaine I tossed any suggestion of this new issue aside, dismissing it as an American buzzword. Bipolar disorder is relatively new in origin, dating back to the late 1950s, so in 2001 drug addicts like myself were still somewhat of a test case.

Opinion is divided as to whether extensive substance abuse can cause bipolar disorder, with the common belief the disorder is already likely to have been there before any cocaine usage started. Furthermore, using cocaine or any other substance is probably a subconscious way of self-medicating.

The extreme bipolar highs and lows and their differing warning signs and symptoms read like the story of my life. Typical traits of the depressive side of the disorder include feeling hopeless, sad and empty; excessive crying; fatigue or loss of energy; sleeping too much or too little; difficulty concentrating and thoughts of death or suicide. On the flip side, common results of the manic side of bipolar are excessive energy; talking too much; poor judgement; out of control spending and aggressive behaviour. The final trait on that side of the spectrum is 'increased sexual activity', but Kevin might have something to say about that. C'mon? We've been married 12 years...so we better change that one to 'increased Twitter activity'.

Seriously, though, we'll never know if I would have experienced all those emotions without cocaine addiction. But I do know that I have been and done all those things since. Getting past everything I've been through is a constant battle. Hiding myself away in my bedroom and sleeping is something I've always done to try and cope. When I was using, if I had caned it for three days, I could sleep for two days straight. I've had the Fire Brigade round at my place before, because friends were so worried about me.

When Kevin and I were on our last break in 2012, and the bipolar disorder kicked in fully, I could function perfectly in terms of getting the kids up and out to school, but I'd be back home and in bed again by 10am. I'd sleep right through until 2pm, then be up again to collect the kids from school. Once their homework and dinner was done I'd be in my PJs again by 7pm. When I'm in that bipolar cycle it feels like a prison sentence and because that time Kevin wasn't around there was nobody to try and snap me out of it.

I still have comedowns now and then, like when I first read back parts of this book, or after I've been working on an exciting project. It's normal for people in everyday life to experience the same feelings, perhaps after a holiday or a really good weekend, when they're suddenly back at work on a Monday morning, but with bipolar those feelings are doubled and trebled and can happen when you least expect it. Kevin and I have both been through so much therapy that he knows the right things to say, but it still takes time to register.

We can each only deal with our own circumstances in isolation, and use any good fortune we do have or have had to help put things into perspective. I'm so fortunate that during spells when I can't be dragged out of bipolar, that I am able to take a tablet to deal with it, and that Kevin is on hand to coax me through the darkest moments. There are so many people with cancer and other incurable diseases who don't have medication they can take. That's how I try to remind myself how selfish sitting in bipolar or not dealing with it can be. I have to tell myself I am not special and that I can be in control.

19
BACK ON SET

The next phase of my acting career came like a bolt out of the blue. One Sunday night I got a call via *Hollyoaks* producer Bryan Kirkwood, who I had worked under for just six weeks during my last stint on *EastEnders*. I must have made some kind of impression, because he was introducing a new character at short notice, and he wanted me to start filming in Liverpool the following week.

With our financial situation at the time, precarious at best, the call came as a real blessing. I knew it meant I could stop claiming benefits. I said I was very interested in the role, but asked if I could check about the repercussions of joining another soap. I was told by the powers that be at *EastEnders* that it would not affect my chances of ever returning to play Sam Mitchell, and, if anything, was encouraged to take the part.

Within days I was on set working, playing ex-jailbird Trudy Ryan, but I quickly realised that *Hollyoaks* was so out of my comfort zone. I could walk back into Albert Square tomorrow and play Sam Mitchell. But this was my first day and I hadn't had a first day in years. Even though I've been doing *EastEnders* for years I was still so scared when I first walked on set. Fortunately the longest running star in the show Nick Pickard, who plays Tony, was on hand to make me a welcoming cup of tea. I've known him since he was nine-years-old, when we were at the Sylvia Young Theatre School together. He relaxed the situation perfectly, and that's when I also met Claire Cooper, who plays Jacqui McQueen. She would be central to my role in the show. She's so lovely and we immediately clicked.

That first day we started at 7.45am, and I was only meant to shoot one scene. We ended up doing five. Everything was just so chilled. All shot on one camera, as if you're doing a drama. And because it's single camera, you end up doing everything about eight times...the scene itself, then wide shots and all our individual close-ups, and some reverse shots too. Nick and Claire were both so unselfish, and gave as much to my shots, as their own.

The crew are very cool and lots of the cast are straight out of drama college. It's a very happy go lucky environment. Brian is a great governor to work for. As well as *EastEnders*, he had a spell on Corrie and then came back to *Hollyoaks*, where he worked earlier in his career. He's constantly talking to people and his door is always open. He's not set in his ways, regimented or untouchable. He's firm, but fair and gets to know everybody.

I got a good feeling about *Hollyoaks*, and the Liverpool area in general, and I knew instinctively I'd be happy to do as much as they wanted me to. As I was travelling up from Essex for my initial stint, and staying at a serviced apartment for a few days at a time, it made a big difference knowing things would be so relaxed when I got there. It was the first time I had worked away, and stayed away on my own, probably since *Ghost Towns*, so it was a big deal for all the family, but we were thankfully in the best place possible to deal with that now.

The people in Liverpool and Manchester seem a lot less judgmental and pretentious than many in London. It's a very close-knit community up there. People are used to having soap stars and footballers around, and give them space. If they had offered me a longer contract, I'd have taken it and probably moved the family up there. I looked at the theatre schools in Liverpool, and I think I'd be more happy for Jodie B to attend one up there than in London. And with Kevin's plans to work in the community or for the church, I'm sure there would be plenty of opportunities for him too.

However, with Trudy's role quickly coming to a natural conclusion, so many other opportunities came out of being on *Hollyoaks*. Suddenly it made sense to stay down south again.

One thing's for sure, I had a blessing when *Hollyoaks* came up, and I'll never say never about a return if the scriptwriters are able to work their magic. It allowed me to play a much grittier role than I'm used to with Sam so I feel blessed that I was able to showcase as someone else, after being a Mitchell for so long. It was great to get back on set, and back acting after so much time away. The feedback I got was so positive, and that meant a lot. I left *Hollyoaks* brimming with confidence, full of hope for the future and excited about my career prospects.

I love the fact anything is possible right now. I never know when the phone will ring or what offer I will receive. When I was promoting my role on *Hollyoaks*, I was a guest panelist for one day for Matthew Wright's daily panel show on Channel 5, and also appeared on *This Morning*. Both invited me back, with *The Wright Stuff* asking me to step-up and be a resident panelist for a week. I love appearing in that format. I've been a guest on *Loose Women* before, and I'd love to do that again. Witnessing Sharon Osbourne first hand working on *The Talk* in the States has inspired me all the more on that front.

I've definitely got the acting bug back too. There are a couple of film scripts I'm currently thinking over, so there could be exciting times ahead on that front. After previously playing *Peter Pan* in Devon and appearing in *Beauty & The Beast* in Canterbury, I also signed up to do panto again for Christmas 2013 - *Dick Whittington* in York - with my mate Danny Young and Chloe Madeley, which I know will be great fun.

In preparation for panto, and in the run up to my 40th birthday the month before, I got back into the gym, and lost a stone in weight in the first month. Kevin would be off to the gym and I'd be sat there with a large bag of Kettle crisps and a bottle of full fat Coke. I'd lost a lot of the weight I put on with my first course of bipolar tablets, but I just started grazing on the sofa. I felt so lethargic. Kevin said: "Your diet sucks, you don't do any exercise and you're the wrong side of 30."

Harsh words, but it worked. After a break from the gym himself, Kevin had quickly got into shape, and it was the kick up the backside I needed. When your husband is a few years older than you and looking great and you're laid out on the sofa watching Jeremy Kyle with a plate of crumpets, it gets to the point when you need to do something about it. Now I'm at the gym as much as I possibly can be...preferably five mornings a week. Having great friends to work out with definitely helps. There's Jo Wheatley, aka Trigga, who used to work for Premier. I persuaded her to move out to Essex from Bermondsey. Then there are the two Suzis...Suzi Swift and Susan Canlas...all great girls.

We're often joined in our normal gym sessions by Will Barnes, our zumba teacher. He's got so much energy and is bundles of fun. Working out with Kevin and the gang means there's never a dull moment and we all spur each other on. It's so important to train with friends or a trainer. When we started the zumba we spent so much time banging into each other, but now we're much more in time. My fellow Essex girl Jodie Marsh got in touch on Twitter when she saw I was back training again, and asked if I'd like to try her workout supplements. I gave some a go and have to say Jodie's Semtex tablets are great for a boxercise or body pump class, or if you've got a really heavy gym session planned. She is so dedicated with her own training, and has reinvented herself through her bodybuilding. Jodie's work on anti-bullying has been amazing too.

Like Jodie Marsh, I'm happy if my fame enables me to highlight a whole host of issues. In particular, I'd like to work with kids who parents are drug addicts, and I'd love to be accepted as a foster parent. Since I made my desire to foster public I had some initial meetings with the BBC about a fly-on-the-wall documentary focussing on the whole process. With my checkered past, I may not seem like the obvious candidate, but it is my dream to become a foster parent. I've not been the best mum in the world, when I was using, and not even in my sobriety, because of the money I lavished on my kids for the wrong reasons. However, I believe I would be going into fostering for the right reasons. We don't want any more kids of our own, but it would be great to provide a home for a child who needed it, and then when it was able and ready, give that child the best chance to return to its own family.

Now the big issue is whether I would ever be accepted as a foster parent, because of my addiction in the past and my bipolar disorder diagnosis. One social worker friend who works for social services says I pretty much possess all the skills and experiences that are needed. It's true a lot of children who need fostering have parents with their own addiction issues.

I believe the main goal with foster care is to get the child back to their family. When I was in the depth of my addiction, before I met Kevin, if someone had given me that opportunity, to have Kai taken into a decent home for three months, I would have bitten their hand off. I called social services. As a very last resort, I tried, but they wouldn't take me seriously. I'd take a child for three months or seven years, whatever it took, whatever was needed. They would still have their parents, but they would be part of our family too, and be treated as our own, while they were in our care.

If I am accepted, then I will be delighted, but I also hope it will encourage other people to get into fostering who maybe assume they would not be accepted for one reason or another. So many children need the help, and the foster parents can get so much from it themselves. I've certainly got the drive and determination to do it, as has Kevin, and we've had some initial consultation meetings. We've chatted to our kids, who are fine with it, so now it's a question of seeing where we will settle next, and what red tape comes up in the meantime.

I do want to highlight certain issues surrounding fostering, and would love to become an ambassador for it, but I'm still not sure a documentary is the best way forward. I think it would have to focus on the process itself, and wouldn't be fair on any children involved if they were over exposed. At the time of writing that project is currently on hold.

Right now, I guess, our priority is getting ourselves back on our feet, and making sure we have a stable base and future from which to build on.

If I'm accepted or not for fostering I can still continue with the various pieces of voluntary work I do, whether it's teaching at Danny Young's drama school in Brentwood, where it's great to work with the young hopefuls there, or at the Pillion Trust homeless shelter in Caledonian Road in north London. Pillion was set up by Savas Panas, who used to be a big cheese in the record business. He specialises in late teens who have lost their way. Savas apparently put all his own kids through university, and told them: "That's your inheritance, I'm spending the rest of my money on the shelter." He's an amazing guy, and I've spent several days there, talking to the kids, trying to give them any advice I can.

I'm always quite picky about the charities that I do work with, but I'd also like to do as much as I can for the elderly too. I think we could all devote more time to senior citizens who don't have anyone. And that's what annoys me about a lot of churches that I've come across in the UK, that they're more about maintaining the church itself, the upkeep of it, rather than helping in the local community.

As much as I want to help other people, there is still lots of work for us do with our own family unit at home. For the first time in my life I feel I've finally got a relationship with my mum...the sort a mother and daughter should have. When we came back from LA I wasn't really talking to her. Kai had come second place in the junior worlds in jiu jitsu, and I thought: "Shit, I can't ring Mum and tell her." And, you know, life's too short for her not to be in contact with her grandchildren. Mum helped us so much in 2012. She got us a little car, she helped when Kevin was ill, and was just generally there for me.

It was Kevin, when he was back with us, who went and met my mum, had lunch with her and tried to build bridges. Considering how instrumental I'd been in severing his ties with his family, that was big of him. He may not have a relationship with his own family, but he tried to patch up issues with mine. It's complicated, like all families, but we have to look at it as one big family, not mine and his, and whoever is in it at the time.

I have had periods when I haven't been on good terms with my mum, and I know I've put her through hell, but I feel so lucky to have had her in my life for so much of it. When we had Gads Hill House she got to spend so much time with the kids, and be a part of them growing up. My dad, bless him, I'm still very close to him too.

Then there's my younger brother Jay. He has simply been my anchor over the years. Sure, Kevin, as my husband is and should be my first port of call, but I'll also go to my brother if I'm having a bad time. It's well documented that my brother is a police officer. I jokingly call him 'Sarge', and having a sister like me as he tried to progress in the force was clearly not ideal at all. We have the same DNA, but he'll have a beer and a curry on a Friday night with his mates, and he's happy. He's never touched drugs, never even had a fag, or brought any trouble to my mum's door.

Much of Jay's childhood was ruined because when he was growing up I had started in *EastEnders* and it was all about me. And it's pretty much been all about me ever since. He would get beaten up at school, like Kai, because of me. It sounds weird, but, for some reason, that's what kids do. Having a sibling who is a celebrity must be hard enough anyway, let alone one who is a well known junkie when you're trying to earn your stripes in the police.

The best thing about my brother is that he tells me how it is. So many people tell me what I want to hear. I can slag Kevin off to Jay and he'll listen, but he'll usually tell me I'm wrong. He won't bitch about Kevin like I want him to at that time. He knows Kevin is usually right, and after witnessing all my other relationships, he knows Kevin is who I should be with.

Kevin has strong beliefs about the children of celebrities. He's sure they grow up thinking they're famous too. They see their parents going out earning large sums of money during an apparently short space of time, or a few grand for a single photoshoot, and they think that's how it's going to be for them. And he's probably right to a certain degree. The trick is trying to find a balance. Kids in general these days are constantly generating their own fame on Facebook and Twitter or on their own YouTube channels. Kevin says they don't even need to be in a reality show, that some of them are starring in their very own reality shows in their heads.

In Kai's case, he's been in the public eye all his life. He's got more than 2,000 Twitter followers, and loads of those were from when his picture flashed up when I was on *The Jeremy Kyle Show*. Women of all ages were tweeting me saying how good looking he is, and that's bound to have an affect. When we were in LA, Kai was pictured coming out of The Sanctuary with a mohawk and a story appeared in one of the tabloids, fuelled by an estranged relative, that he had joined a cult in California, and that just doesn't happen to your average kid.

Kai's my mate and I love him so much, but there is always bound to be this complicated bond between us. I look at him and, because of what we went through together, as his parent, I always feel so guilty. Back in my darkest days when I was using, I was empty, and felt I couldn't show Kai the love he deserved. Then in the years of luxury that followed, I look back and think I bought him rather than loved him. When I stopped using

I often felt so detached and I now realise at times I have compensated in the wrong ways. It all adds to my guilt. It's time to be honest because honesty in our family is vital for us now, and something we all insist on. We are always evolving, and evaluating. The job is never done.

Kai has always been very confident. He's been around adults all his life. When Kevin first met him he was only two yet he was so opinionated, and still is. With Kai about to leave school and approaching his late teens, having a child of that age is always a worry. You have to let them have their freedom, but you never stop worrying about the choices that they make. All you can do is be there for them.

Jodie B is our little free spirit. She is so strong, so caring and totally infectious. She feels people's hurt and pain. I was using crack when Jodie was conceived so we really do see her as our little miracle. At times Jodie has been the glue that has held us together. Just one of her smiles can cut the tension, and change the mood. I believe she is an unusual child, in that when she says sorry, she genuinely means it. Jodie's a bit of an old hippy, and I think spending time in LA when she was so young has influenced that. She's also got an amazing voice, so watch this space...you heard it here first.

Because we have moved so much Jodie has attended various schools. I kept her down a year last year, because she had some catching up to do. When she was at private school in Kent, she was told she was dyslexic and partially deaf. She had two ear ops when she was little and she's fine now, but she couldn't get a lot of the work. Then again, she was doing I.T, French and German, and she was only four. I tried to put my kids through the best education around, but at times it was like trying to put a square peg in a round hole.

When we came back from LA, Jodie specifically asked if she could go to the village school, and within three months there, she'd caught up on all subjects. The pressure was off, and she improved. Kevin's eldest daughter Jordan is a great big sister to both of our kids. Kai listens to her, and Jodie has a special relationship with Jordan too.

Sure, the luxury that the kids enjoyed when they were growing up was great to a point. They've known times when they've had everything, but have had a lot of hard times too. They've gone from first class travel all over the world to mum signing on and struggling to put food on the table. They've experienced highs and lows and I think that's such good grounding for them.

For better or worse, after seeing so many people turn us over, they've also learned a lot about trust and expectations. Personally, I don't think that can be a bad thing. If my kids have learned a lot of life's lessons along the way, and the whole experience has taught them that at least they have got each other, that we've all got each other, then I've got no complaints.

Importantly, Kai and Jodie have learned that the world doesn't have to be a material one. Over the years the kids had quad bikes and go-carts for Christmas presents. Last year, Kai was choked when he opened a pair of Nike Airmax trainers, because he didn't think he was going to get them. And that made me happier than all the stupidly expensive gifts I've ever given him. I learned so much in that year, and I'm in such a good space because of it. I've learned the hard way, but I'll still be shopping at Asda and checking out the Tesco value range, and heading to Primark when I can. I won't be dropping those places any day soon.

I only came off benefits when I got my fee through from *The Jeremy Kyle Christmas Special* and my two-month stint on *Hollyoaks* was confirmed. Sure, I'd like to kit Kai and Jodie out in loads of nice clothes, but we've been there, done that and got too many designer T-Shirts! It does hurt because I've made a load of mistakes along the way, and I feel so guilty at times. It's the little things now that can mean so much. Kai and I spent some time together at Westfield in Stratford recently, walking around the shops, looking at what we wished we could buy, and I can honestly say it was much more enjoyable wishing than simply grabbing and getting it all. As a result we spent a lot more quality time together in the process.

We've always been honest with the kids, and told them everything they need to know on an age-appropriate basis. You can't say they will never take drugs because our parents thought we would never take them. Certain things in life shape you, and your kids certainly do. You start to see yourself in them as they're growing up and it makes you judge and think about yourself. Eventually, with both Kai and Jodie, just like my addictions, it may well be a case of tough love. A case of, if you love them set them free. We do believe in our kids making their own mistakes. Hopefully their's won't be even ten per cent as bad as ours.

20
CLARITY

When my first book came out I was already in a whole heap of trouble. It was hailed as a success story and, of course, beating my terrible addiction to cocaine was a huge triumph. However, the timeline tails off around 2004, and by the time it came out the Bilton liaisons and *Ghost Towns* party had happened. I felt my life was a mess.

On the face of it, everything was rosy, but, if possible, I was hiding away for two days at a time, hoping that nothing came out in the press. All I could do was hold tight and pray nothing hit the *News Of The World* or any of the other red tops.

People will say that I was only thinking about income from book sales, and they would be right to a certain degree. Money was such a massive part of my life, almost as big an addiction as my extraordinary drug habit. When the first book did come out, my life of luxury was not touched on. If Bilton or *Ghost Towns* hit the press, as the Bilton one eventually did, I couldn't be sure Kevin wouldn't leave again.

In the years previously...2002/03/04...I had been riding on the wave of getting clean. I'll admit, I had a very high opinion of myself because I had kicked drugs. At that age, with my status...the house, the cars, two lovely kids and a loyal and devoted husband...I thought I had it all. Well, I've still got the kids and the husband, and now I realise all the material things don't matter in comparison. The first book was as honest as I could be, pre my bipolar being fully diagnosed and treated. I was very clear about my addiction, and how I beat it, and the depths I had often plunged during that period, but couldn't and didn't know how to reveal and deal with the underlying issues which had prolonged my addictions.

Five years later, in 2009, when Kevin confronted me in the run-up to my *EastEnders* comeback and my appearance on *Dancing On Ice*, I thought: "OK, you've been riding your luck for so long," and that was the beginning of the end of my self-imposed life sentence. It was as if I didn't start working on the relationship until it looked like I could lose everything, and at the exact point when I had the most to lose.

When working on this book I'd lost the lot, and surely me going even deeper this time is no coincidence. I was ready to be honest, but I didn't ever think I would be this honest and publicly talk about such delicate issues. When I started these book sessions the big house had gone, our beautiful lifestyle in LA was a distant memory and Kevin and I had only just got back together again for the umpteenth time. But this time it was different. I'd hit my own rock bottom, and just off housing benefit, I was juggling the dole queue with an unlikely TV comeback.

While talking about the 1994 abduction was so cleansing at the time, when I sat down to read it back after my stint on *Hollyoaks* it was so much harder. I hadn't planned to talk about it during that particular session, but it suddenly just felt right, and it came out. It was tough, I was in tears, but I also felt like a huge weight had been lifted from my shoulders. I felt lighter and younger again, just like at Cottonwood.

However, when reading it back it was suddenly so vivid again, and I struggled so much after that. I had just finished a load of high profile TV interviews. There had been a front page story in The Sun about my plans to foster, and when I sat down to start proof-reading the book I came crashing back down to earth. In between sessions over those next few weeks I struggled badly. I didn't do any housework for a fortnight, didn't pick up the hoover, just did basics like the washing and cooking. That's when bipolar disorder can come to the surface again, and if I'm not on top of it, mentally and medication-wise, then that's when it can take over.

Looking back around the time of that drug debt made me regret not dealing with certain issues earlier, wondering if I had dealt with what happened in 1994 in treatment how different things would have been over the last 20 years. I surely would have been a different mother, wife and person. I was only 21 at the time. It's so frightening looking back. It's like that ordeal has held me captive all this time, that I've been a prisoner within my own life. Towards the end of writing this book, going back through everything again ruined me, but at least this time I wasn't glossing over anything. I found it so hard even getting out of bed again.

It's been so tough for Kevin, but at least he now knows so much more about what I'd buried. I really thought I would take those things to my grave. I also told my mum for the first time too, and she was understandably horrified. Her first reaction was: "Why the hell didn't you call me?" I explained I simply felt there was no way I could turn up on her doorstep with those people. I've since somehow had to reassure her that it's over now and dealt with.

And I was dealing with it. Slowly but surely the clarity came through. I started to clean the house, and clear out a load of old rubbish, designer clothes that I had held on to, which only served to remind me of traumatic times in my life. I've had to take so many steps back, just to take a few vital steps forward.

When *The Sunday People* splashed the leak of my abduction on their front page it was so hard for all of us. It came out in April 2012, four or five weeks before the newspaper serialisation in the run-up to the publication of this book. It was now well and truly out, and a case of dealing with it the best we could. I have to admit, with the headline screaming "DANNIELLA KIDNAP & RAPE BY DRUGS GANG" I felt like a piece of meat again. The article said I was held at gunpoint, which was not actually the case, and explained I would be revealing all in my new autobiography. It obviously brought everything to the forefront of my mind again, and, of course, I had doubts about whether I was doing the right thing.

Even though I knew I was talking about the abduction for the correct reasons, it still made me wonder if I was making a mistake. I've long known that going back over these events could mean the police would want to get involved, and interview me about what happened. This whole process has meant that I have had to waive my right to lifetime anonymity as a victim of a sexual attack, so the police may come knocking. I would be happy to cooperate. However, I either do not know or simply cannot remember the people involved. Any recollection of them was systematically erased from my memory, either through excessive cocaine use since, what I was given during the whole ordeal or because it was the only way of coping.

It has, of course, been particularly hard for Kevin. He had given me the choice to wipe my slate clean and got more than he bargained for. He could just about deal with my wrap party revelation, and we very nearly divorced over that, but he wasn't ready then for any details of the abduction. He naturally cannot bear the thought of anyone harming me, let alone a sexual assault of that kind.

We saw The Sunday People front page together on Sky News late on the Saturday night and for Kevin it suddenly became real. He still didn't know much about it, and refused to read that chapter of this book. It's his way of coping, but the main thing is that he now knows, and I know he knows.

But now the children had to know too. This was my life before I had children, and it's obviously difficult talking to them about any of it. I know if I wasn't in the public eye, things wouldn't come out like this, and so when anything does appear in the papers I always feel guilty that I have put the kids and Kevin in the spotlight once more. Kai seemed to take it OK, but then understandably got more angrier throughout the day, and started asking lots of questions. We sat Jodie down and told her I'd got beaten up a little bit, but she gave me a big hug and said: "Mum, don't worry, I heard you talking about it late last night. I've already googled it, I know what happened." Bless her.

I'm sure I will be judged over these latest revelations, but I'm used to that.

Within minutes of *The Sunday People* story breaking, differing comments appeared on my Twitter feed. Someone quickly replied: "You are very brave, take time out for yourself", but then the first troll appeared with: "You going to rehab you raving bugle addict?". "Just seen the front of the Sunday People, hope you're OK?" was next up, closely followed by "I bet you enjoyed getting raped you slapper, you deserved it." Other tweets are simply too vile to print, including one disgusting and degrading message, it appeared, from a female.

Those who hate me will probably always hate me, but those that do like me, usually do so because I'm a normal working class girl they can relate to. I can do the PR actress Danniella bit, but I'm normally very open with whoever I meet. I needed to get this out, for myself, and so, hopefully, a few other people don't waste long parts of their lives, burying things that need to be dealt with, or being a prisoner to something that they can one day get past. I now know I'm a strong person, and I'd love other people to find strength too. It's tough, but I can deal with it. The time has come when I don't have to beat myself up over everything.

Twitter isn't all bad. I was skipping round the kitchen the day David Walliams followed me. I'm a massive fan of his, and we have a mutual friend in comedian Ian Royce. David sent me a Direct Message, asking if I remembered sharing a cab with him after an event in 1993. I was so chuffed, but had to point out I can't remember much of 1993 at all. I have more than 70,000 followers on Twitter, but I can get as starstruck as the next person.

Of course, Social Media can be counter-productive at times, but a lot of positive things come out of it too. There's a lot of fun to be had bantering with friends and loads of great causes are highlighted and get support. It's a case of taking the rough with the smooth where

Twitter and Facebook is concerned, and always being mindful of their limitations and the pitfalls involved.

At the time of going to print I have been clean from cocaine for 12 years, but as long as I live in the UK the stigma of my addiction will never leave me. I've had a few wake-up calls in my life, but I received another large one only weeks before this book was published. I let my guard down and the papers had a field day. One article contained a whole host of photos and a headline which commented: '*Danniella Westbrook appears worse for wear as she leaves G-A-Y bar after hours inside*'. The piece began: "She's a self-confessed drug addict who has been clean 12 years. But it seems Danniella Westbrook may have fallen off the alcohol wagon on Tuesday night when she emerged from a bar..."

I will hold my hands up and admit, yes, I did have a few drinks, but then so did thousands of people in Soho that night. I have never said I was on the "alcohol wagon". I was in a cab on my way home by 9.30pm, so it was hardly the "wild night out" that another tabloid talked about. Their headline "Danni's EastBender" was predictable, if nothing else, but also a little way off the mark. Time was, a wild night out for me was getting home at 9.30am, or 9.30pm the next night!

This "wild night out" began when I arrived in central London at around 8am for a TV interview and a series of meetings regarding this book. I'd had a tough couple of days since the details of the abduction appeared in *The*

Sunday People, so after what had been a busy, but productive day I suggested to Kevin that we grab a quick drink. After a long and punishing winter it happened to be one of the sunniest evenings of the year so far. There was a buzz in the air, and I clearly needed to let my hair down. However, with my hair peroxide blonde, and wearing my garish leopard print coat, Kevin reckons I looked like a Belisha Beacon, not to mention Trudy Ryan, my brassy character in *Hollyoaks*. We headed to Balans in Old Compton Street, a favourite restaurant of mine. It had been an intensive four or five months working on this project, so we ordered some food and a couple of drinks. Later I hooked up with my agent and we spent a couple of hours at the G.A.Y bar further down Old Compton Street. Yes, I had a few more drinks in G.A.Y and, yes, I was a bit tipsy, but if this was a "wild night out" then nobody invited me. By 10pm I was snoozing in the cab and almost home.

In reality, I know the score well enough. I know I can't be walking (or stumbling) around Soho, certainly not looking and dressed as I was. If I light up a cigarette, the papers will comment. If I have a few drinks, then they will always try to link it to my old cocaine addiction. It's not fair, but I appreciate it comes with the territory, and certainly my territory. I do realise as a known drug addict I now can't be seen in public tottering out of a bar or a club, whatever time of the day.

One paper claimed I have "also battled the booze", when, in reality, I've never had a drink problem. In truth, I've never been able to drink that much. Sure, the more I took cocaine, the more I drank (and smoked), but any cocaine user will tell you the three often go hand in hand. I have picked up a glass of wine on the odd occasion since my recovery in 2001, and usually during a split with Kevin. I didn't drink at all in LA, for instance, but I'll admit that I did start drinking again occasionally when we returned to the UK, and when Kevin had his meltdown and moved out for those few months. If I'm honest, it was a year from hell for me. I didn't want to leave LA, but I did so to support my husband.

The outcry after these seemingly innocent drinks with friends in Soho reminded me I just cannot put myself in this kind of position any more. The next day I had another moment of clarity, and resolved to act more responsibly in the future. I can have a couple of drinks with my friends at home, or in the village pub even, but not in Soho. I'm a notorious drug addict, and I'm fair game for a lot of people. I was beating myself up the next day, and it's harder than ever to move on now. The old saying about today's newspapers being tomorrow's chip paper doesn't ring true anymore. Everything is online now, and remains so...an indelible footprint that's impossible to delete.

Ironically, my schedule that day had started with David Grant interviewing me for the BBC's Songs Of Praise show in Piccadilly Circus. Kevin reckons the whole episode was God's way of reminding me how potentially vulnerable I am, that it was as if he was saying: "Right, you can have this, the 'falling out of a bar Danniella', or you can check yourself and become fully focussed again.

The reality is I'll never escape my past. There's even a punk metal band called Daniella Westbrook...spelt incorrectly with only one 'n', by the way. Their PR blurb states: "Formed accidentally in early 2010 out of a combination of sheer boredom and ketamine." Well, yep, I've been there, and done that too.

I've come to believe that other people's opinions, what they think of me, is none of my business. You can't let it get you down. It did used to bother me. I'd read all the negative tweets and press, but once I was officially being treated for bipolar disorder I wasn't bothered. There are so many haters on Twitter, but I just block them, and move on. Those cowardly trolls used to spoil my day, but not now. There's only so many times someone can tweet you something like: "Oi, cokewhore, how's your beak?" and it bothers you. You just get used to blocking them and ignoring it. My attitude is that if they haven't got anything better to do with their lives, then that's their look-out. The odd bad tweet is nothing compared to what some people have to deal with daily, people with incurable diseases for instance. It doesn't even compare. I don't read the papers or magazines any more, unless there's an article I collaborated on, or a specific interview I've given. I used to collect everything that was written about me, but not any more. I'm more worried about what we're having for dinner than what people are saying about me.

My faith has helped me be more pragmatic about my fame and the notoriety that comes with it, and the addiction that has caused me so many problems over the years. While I believe Kevin is a wholly good person, I often feel so worthless. Kevin is very open spiritually. I think I used to be a spiritually open person all those years ago before I touched drugs and surrounded myself with so much crap. The more people thought I was lowlife, the more I immersed myself in darker circles. I took cocaine during both pregnancies. I lied, cheated, stole and have been unfaithful. I mean, how many commandments do you want to break? Just like I have had to pray for forgiveness, we've also prayed for forgiveness for anyone in our past who turned us over. You ask God to put the lightness in, and take the darkness out...and I think only God can fix that part of your heart. When I first went to The Sanctuary and discovered my faith, I really wanted it and I felt so uplifted, but I just couldn't believe I would ever be truly accepted, that God would ever forgive me for all of that little lot.

My faith is definitely a work in progress so I need to take it a step at a time. I can find Kevin's faith quite overpowering at times...he got it so much more quickly than me. There's no doubt my faith has helped with the guilt, but there is a stigma attached to it, the 'God Squad' and all that, particularly where the media is concerned. It's seems every time I have spoken about my faith I get a lot of negative press as well. Various people in the UK have approached us to get involved in their churches, but we're not involved with a specific one at the moment. That doesn't mean we don't take our faith seriously.

People don't believe it, but we're genuinely happier without the money. We don't miss the house, the cars or the lifestyle. Kevin says he misses running the company, the leadership and troubleshooting, but that being needed didn't get him anywhere in the end. He could start up another company, and may well do one day, and earn another big bag of money, but that will come with another big bag of trouble.

Kevin reckons that falling in love with me stopped him going to prison. That's where he would have ended up. Fortunately, the lies we both told ourselves didn't work anymore. We didn't have the answers. And that's when we found God. Kevin jokes that he asked God: "Please sort out my wife", and that he replied: "You've been playing God to her for the last 12 years."

Up until fairly recently I haven't been happy for any long period of time. The crying never stopped. Kevin always had faith in me, and I don't know why. It can only be love. Since I've been a child it's always been about me. Since I was at stage school, it was me, me, me. Like a talented footballer who the whole family knows is going to make it by the time they're 12-years-old. In my own family, I was the big hope. Like a Gazza or a Frank Bruno. It seems like I've been in the public eye for as long as I can remember.

Kevin reckons that everyone who is on TV is slightly abnormal, and once you get used to people recognising you it sets something off that is impossible to control. It colours the way you react to the world and you look differently at everything from that point onwards. And I think he's right. Fame could just be the strongest addiction anyone can have. Most people want fame, whether they say they do or not. Most people when they've got it, don't know what to do with it, and they either want more or want to get rid of it. It's so easy to think you're special, and Kevin reckons a celeb needs the support of a special person, a special husband, wife or partner too...haha...but then I guess he would say that.

It's true that I am constantly having to check myself and how my fame is affecting me. For instance, Botox hadn't felt necessary for quite a while, but that soon changed when I signed up for *Hollyoaks*. So many celebrities are at it, that it's unusual these days if you're not doing it. It's amazing how being thrust back into the spotlight can see me creeping back to the clinic for a few tactical jabs. It only takes a couple of nasty comments on Twitter about how badly I've aged and I'm back in the chair. However, I think as an actress gets older it's important to age, to have lines and character in your face, so you do have to be careful with Botox.

That said, I have thankfully reached a stage in my life where I don't care if people look at me and say "she's lost her looks because of drugs". I would love them to walk a day in my shoes or go through half of what I have, and still get up each day and get on with their lives. I think eventually I just got bored of being half-empty all the time. I've spent too many nights crying myself to sleep because of nasty things about me in the press or on the internet. You just learn to deal with it better.

Behind all the glamour of celebrity, there is always a big price to fame. Others could come out of rehab, and slip back into society fairly easily. They could get on the tube or go to Tesco without people looking down at them, mumbling "cokehead" under their breaths, making sniffing noises or rubbing their noses. It still happens to me all the time. I'm like, "oh, you're so funny, you're first person to have ever done that." Of course, they don't know me, or the real me. Once I got over myself I found it easier to get over them. And if anyone out there is perfect, then, go ahead, please cast the first stone. Through my faith, I've now realised that, actually, my fame and status can help a lot of good causes, and that's much more important than all the negativity that comes with it.

When I went on the Jeremy Kyle celebrity special people said I was a Z-lister, but it certainly didn't stop journalists ripping loads of quotes from it, and slapping me all over the national newspapers again. Doing the show with Jeremy wasn't a case of wanting to defend myself - I'm past all that. It was more the fulfillment I get from thinking I might just be helping someone else. Let's make no mistake, though, it was also a job and, now more than ever, I need to get paid. You do have to get the balance right. I'm not in *OK Magazine* or *Closer* every week talking about my problems, like others I could mention, and I do turn down a lot of requests for stuff which isn't quite right for me...things that could be counter-productive or seem salacious.

I still take each day as it comes, to a certain extent. Although it's hell at the time, getting clean is the easy part. The hard bit is staying clean, but I'm lucky I haven't thought about taking cocaine since I left Cottonwood...they did such a good job on me. I battled for my life to get clean and, to be honest, the thought of taking cocaine again frightens the crap out of me.

I still get offered coke, though. I was at a concert in Shepherd's Bush recently with a friend and two young girls were talking to us. They were both pretty and in their early 20s. As one headed to the toilets she casually said to me: "Do you want a line?" I politely declined, and she said: "Have I offended you?" I replied: "No, not at all," but I just felt bad for her.

There are loads of people my age taking cocaine on a so-called recreational level. I could never do 'moderation'. I only have one speed when it comes to drugs. Now, after years of being uncontrollable, I love to be in control.

Another time, a few years ago, a well-known celebrity invited Kevin and I up to his hotel room after a showbiz party for a nightcap. We were sitting there, waiting for a vodka tonic or maybe a beer from the mini bar, when he suddenly tipped a gram of coke on a table, and said: "Here you go...this is a good test for you." Kevin nearly knocked him out. The guy knew me well, and was acutely aware of my problems. It was totally irresponsible of him and, as the saying goes, we made our excuses and left.

Getting offered coke is always going to come with my territory, and who am I to complain? I can't have it all. Back in the day, I couldn't get enough of the stuff. It doesn't matter if I did great on *Dancing On Ice*, have another decent stint on *EastEnders* or people like my work on *Hollyoaks*, most will still look at me as 'that cokehead'. The media will always interpret it their own way. When I talked about snorting coke before, during and after Kai's birth on Jeremy Kyle there was a big hoo-hah in the tabloids the next day, when, in fact, it was well documented in my last book. It's either lazy journalism and the reporters haven't done their homework, or they're just too young to remember it all coming out before.

But I don't care if people slate me for talking about it. Personally, I don't think God got me clean to suddenly shut up about it all. If I'm honest, I don't actually think the plan was for me to be an actor. I've grown to understand that clean, I'm a caring person, and I would like to make the most of that going forward. And if my fame helps me do that, then great. If me being brutally honest makes other people think about what they're doing with their lives, then all good. It's a huge cliche, I know, but you have to take the positives from the negatives.

I feel like I've grown into myself, and let my journey be my journey. I've stopped fighting against everything, and that's where my faith comes in. Finally admitting to what happened in that flat in south London, and accepting that the extreme consequences were not my fault, could well be my biggest achievement to date, and means Kevin and I can move forward in a way we've never been able to before. I've simply wore myself out trying to keep one foot in my self-destructive past.

Now, as we look toward the future, we both have an open mind about where we settle. Whether you believe in fate or not, or sliding doors, when life is unpredictable you never know what is around the corner. If we hadn't come back to Essex I wouldn't have met some amazing friends. Cheryl and her husband Michael, in particular, have been such a huge support to me, Kevin and all the family. It's blessing to be around genuine people, who don't have an agenda.

Sometimes you've got to stop looking back...it's in the past for a reason. It's the growing up part where life throws you the curve balls. Then it becomes the survival of the fittest. You get knocked out, so you get up again. You need the highs and lows to appreciate everything you've got. Understand that you messed up, why it happened, keep focussed and move on. I feel immensely lucky that I went into *EastEnders* in my teens, and that I've had all the bad experiences along the way too. I feel extremely fortunate that both my kids are healthy, and that I have a great husband, and a forgiving one at that. At times, I've enjoyed the most amazing lifestyle, and got into the craziest scrapes. As a family we've also shared tough times, and that can only make us stronger.

If we are to move on, both Kevin and I are adamant we should renew our wedding vows. I've broken a few of them since we've been married, and so I need to address that. Since we were saved in LA we have struggled with our Christian life in the UK. We both think we need a fresh start and, to a certain extent, our original vows have been smashed to pieces. Kevin says that God has looked out for us so much that we can't go on testing him forever, and jokes that there is only so much of his wrath we can incur.

We were offered a magazine deal to renew our vows in Las Vegas, but that just didn't feel right. We couldn't imagine doing that in one of those tacky chapels out there. It would be a total sham. Huntington Beach, where we were saved, would be more appropriate and provide an amazing setting, but the chances of all our close family members and friends being able to make it out to LA would be slim. Hosting it at home in the UK somewhere, probably where we currently live in Essex, would make much more sense, and so that's what we're hoping to do. We would love Pastor Jay to officiate at the ceremony. He has married people in LA, so we'll try and see if that is possible. Right now, our faith is so important to us. Kevin says he's still waiting for God to tell him what he has planned for us all next, and is honest enough to admit, some days, he's not even sure there is a plan.

I'd like to be the one out earning the money, and I'd prefer it if Kevin went and worked for the church, did something on a voluntary basis for a while, if that's what it took, before he could earn a living out of it. If Kevin does go back into business one day it would have to be totally on his terms. Recently someone approached him about setting up another dispatch company in central London, or even out of Stansted Airport, which is very close to where we live now. A friend said to me: "You'll have your Range Rovers and Porsches back within in three months and another big house in six months," but I don't want all that again. I thought I wanted it all my life, but now I don't.

I love the day-to-day nature of my life. I don't know what will happen next, just like that call for *Hollyoaks* came completely out of the blue. Life is unpredictable, but there is so much hope. The main thing is that I'm ready. I'd love Kevin to do some work within the community or the church, because he'll be building a legacy not an empire. He's got a wife who can earn a decent living, now she's got focus and, for the first time, clarity in her life. I'll always remember Kevin's therapist, Erol, from The Priory, who I saw a few times. I hated seeing him because he always got the truth out of me, unlike others I could mention. He would say: "Dan...is it going to enhance your life?" In the last couple of years I've finally come to realise what does and what doesn't enhance my life.

My family is the happiest its been. We always were a family, just a dysfunctional one with money. I'm so glad we had our fall when we did. It felt like we shouldn't have been at Gads Hill House and in turn going to LA was simply putting off the inevitable. When you're living the dream on borrowed time, it's like being on a holiday that is slowly running out. You know with each new day you're edging towards the end.

We're now living in the smallest house we've ever had, we haven't got a lot of money and I'm driving a regular car, but I truly feel blessed. Yes, it's been horrific for us, because we were so spoilt, but we're all still standing.

I feel like I'm turning a new chapter, and as I approach 40, that life is just beginning. It's exciting. I believe God has made my new career opportunities possible, and that he wants Kevin to do something much more useful with his time than running another stressful business. My main job now is to maintain some sort of status quo, and to make sure that I'm known much more for the characters that I play or the work that I do, than simply being Danniella Westbrook.

THANK YOU

OK, so where to start? There are so many people to thank for their help and support over the last few years, and with the writing and self-publishing of this book.

First and foremost, Kevin...Without you there would be no book. Thank you for making my life awesome. This would have been a non-starter without your amazing memory. Thanks for talking me round when I wake up and panic about everything. You have helped me make important decisions and taught me how to trust again. You have given me so much strength, love and support and always been so very honest with me. Without you I surely wouldn't have made it. You are the most amazing father, and warrior of God! Thank you for seeing something in me nobody else could - least of all myself. This book allows me to tell the truth. Thanks for never giving up, for holding on, and for being you. Bonnie and Clyde forever, huh? Love you baby! D xxxx

Kai, Jodie B and Jordan...You are the most amazing kids. You'll never know how proud I am of all of you...and always will be...and how much joy you guys give me every day. It cannot be measured. I could burst with pride at the way you are growing up. I'm so blessed to be your mum. Love you...all the world. Mum. xx

Cheryl...Well, Mrs C, I wanna say thanks for all your help with this book...and for being an amazing friend. I truly love ya babe. The constant and endless cups of teas, sandwiches, Chinese takeaways and tears and laughter have helped me more than you can ever imagine. Here's to our next adventure. x

Mum & Dad...Thank you for never being ashamed of me and for loving me even when you must have been so scared of what would happen. I love you both so much. Xxxx

Sarge aka my little brother Jay...I know I bore you silly telling you how proud I am of you, but here we go again... I'm super proud of you...how you have done so well, how you have always been there for me no matter what time of day or night. You're so awesome. I couldn't ask for a better brother. Love you Sarge. xxx

Matt...Working on this book has been like writing a feature length version of *EastEnders*. You have worked so hard and kept me sane through the laughs, tears, tweets, bipolar days and blonde moments. You've done an amazing job sorting stuff out. I know you've had to change this book a zillion times. Still wish the glove box story had made the cut, though...lol...thanks again mate. x

Nicky & Jackie Hunt...Thanks you two for your amazing restaurant. Catch is the best gaff in Essex and, after all the years we've all known each other, it feels like home for us. Thanks so much for hosting the book launch. Here's to many more years and to roly-poly Fridays! x

Jam Deluxe...Huge thanks to Jaysam and Michael for your hard work and support shooting the cover, doing my hair and make-up, and running around on other jobs with me. Thank you so much guys x

Pastor Jay Haizlip...Thank you for The Sanctuary, for showing us the way as new Christians and for being such a great pastor. We miss California and your amazing church.

Christy Hazlip...Thanks for being my 'homie', for our cupcake runs and for teaching me about Jesus. Love you Momma C. x

Lili & Cleber Luciano...You guys are the most genuine, beautiful people in the world, the best friends anyone could ask for. Thank you for everything you have done and for all the love you have shown us. We miss you guys, our gorgeous godson Enzo...the whole family...and love you so much. xxx

DANNIELLA WESTBROOK

Daniella's first book *The Other Side Of Nowhere* was published in 2006 to critical acclaim, and became a 'No 1 Bestseller'. She joined the cast of *EastEnders* in 1990, enjoying, in total, four stints on the flagship BBC1 show...the last in 2009. In 2012 Danniella joined Channel 4 soap opera *Hollyoaks*, and in 2013 became a popular panelist on Channel 5's topical magazine show *The Wright Stuff.*

MATT TROLLOPE

A NCTJ-trained journalist, Matt's career began at The Romford Recorder in 1991. One of his first jobs saw him cover a school fete opened by a certain Danniella Westbrook. He went on to work as a freelance music journalist, and within the dance music industry. He is also the author of *The Life & Lines Of Brandon Block* and *One More - A History of UK Clubbing, 1988 - 2008.*

3882635R00152

Printed in Great Britain
by Amazon.co.uk, Ltd.,
Marston Gate.